A TEACHER'S HANDBOOK FOR CONTEXTUAL CLASSROOM COMMUNICATION

DR. M. RATCHAGAR

Fondly dedicate this resourceful book to my sisters

M.Jackuline Mary

M.Leema Rose

M.Regina Mary

Contents

Preface

I have often been urged by my sisters, who are teachers, to help them improve their English. They have a strong desire to gain proficiency in the language. Having studied in a vernacular medium, they are deeply motivated to speak English fluently. Frequently, they call me to clarify doubts regarding sentence usage, word choice, or grammatical structures. Occasionally, they even chide me for not helping them learn spoken English.

I am presenting this book to assist countless other teachers who aspire to master English and to support them in developing the language skills necessary for effective classroom communication. It serves as a comprehensive solution to the communication needs of teachers. The book addresses a wide range of contexts in which communication occurs between teachers and students, colleagues, principals, and other officials. It is both a practical guide and a valuable resource that teachers can rely on throughout their professional journey.

Dr.M.Ratchagar

Acknowledgements

I thank my father, Mr. N. Mahimaidoss, and my mother, Mrs. M. Anthonyammal, for the selfless love, care, and affection showered on me throughout my life.

I extend my heartfelt gratitude to my elder brother, Mr. M. Augustine, for motivating me and consistently supporting and guiding me in all my endeavours.

I also sincerely thank my elder brother, Mr. M. Stephen Raj, for his guidance and support.

I thank my uncles, Mr.C.Jayaraj, Mr. C.John Bosco, and Mr. R.Selvakumar

I am delighted to convey my gratitude to Sanjay, Jeni, Rand, Roshney, Rene, Ryan, Reya, Joshuva, Rheayona, and Raphael

I am grateful to R. Indumathi and S. Kalaiselvi for the technical support rendered by them.

CHAPTER ONE

CONTEXTUAL CLASSROOM COMMUNICATION

Before the Assembly

1. Good morning, everyone.
2. Please stand in line.
3. Walk quietly to the assembly area.
4. Make sure you are in your class line.
5. No talking while we walk.
6. Stay with your group.
7. Let's move in an orderly manner.
8. Is everyone here?
9. Wait for the signal to move.
10. Keep your hands to yourself.
11. Face forward, please.
12. Keep your voice low.
13. The assembly will start shortly.
14. Listen carefully to the announcements.
15. Clap only when appropriate.
16. Show respect during the national anthem.
17. Don't push or run.
18. Let's represent our class well.
19. Be attentive and respectful.
20. Return quietly after the assembly.

21. Form a straight line.
22. Don't bring any food or drink.
23. Hold your belongings properly.
24. Help your classmates if needed.
25. Remain silent during prayers.
26. Smile and stand confidently.
27. Respond when your name is called.
28. No mobile phones allowed.
29. Wear your ID card properly.
30. Remember to behave politely.
31. Don't distract others.
32. Be proud of your school.
33. Let's stay focused.
34. Look attentive on stage.
35. Don't fidget or move around.
36. Listen to the guest speaker.
37. Don't laugh or whisper.
38. Sit down only when instructed.
39. Maintain discipline throughout.
40. Be a role model for others.
41. Applaud when it's appropriate.
42. Encourage your classmates.
43. Follow the teacher's lead.
44. Don't lean on the railings.
45. Look after younger students.
46. Take the shortest route quietly.
47. Keep your uniform neat.
48. Wait patiently for instructions.
49. Always stay alert.
50. Be ready to return to class silently.

During the Assembly

1. Stand still, please.
2. Eyes to the front.
3. Listen carefully to the speaker.
4. Keep your hands by your side.
5. Maintain silence.

6. Show respect during prayers.
7. Sing the anthem with pride.
8. Do not talk to your neighbor.
9. Pay attention to the announcements.
10. Clap only when asked.
11. Let's show our discipline.
12. Watch your posture.
13. No whispering.
14. Stay focused.
15. Look at the stage.
16. Remain calm and quiet.
17. Be respectful to all speakers.
18. Appreciate the performance quietly.
19. Follow the school protocol.
20. Observe proper decorum.
21. Stay in your line.
22. Support your fellow students.
23. Don't fidget.
24. No unnecessary movements.
25. Wait for your turn to perform.
26. Speak clearly if you are presenting.
27. Maintain eye contact with the audience.
28. Use the microphone properly.
29. Greet the audience before speaking.
30. Thank the speaker with applause.
31. Wait for the next announcement.
32. Keep your ID card visible.
33. Keep your feet together while standing.
34. Avoid yawning or stretching.
35. Represent your class well.
36. Applaud politely.
37. Participate with enthusiasm.
38. Show leadership.
39. Set a good example.
40. Don't chew gum.
41. Keep your belongings safe.
42. Look proud and confident.
43. Wait for dismissal instructions.

44. Do not crowd the exit.
45. Allow the front rows to move first.
46. Walk silently back to class.
47. Keep the assembly area clean.
48. Reflect on the message shared.
49. Smile when appropriate.
50. Thank the guests before leaving.

Starting the Class

1. Open your books.
2. Close your books.
3. Take out your notebooks.
4. Put your books away.
5. Pay attention, please.
6. Listen carefully.
7. Look at the board.
8. Write this down.
9. Read the sentence aloud.
10. Let's begin.
11. Shall we start?
12. Are you ready to begin?
13. Today we are going to learn about...
14. Turn to page 10.
15. Who's absent today?
16. Let's review what we did last time.
17. Please settle down.
18. Is everyone here?
19. Let's start with a warm-up activity.
20. Please sit down.

Group and Pair Work
21. Work in pairs.
22. Work in groups.
23. Find a partner.
24. Take turns.

25. Share your answers.
26. Discuss with your group.

Worksheet and Textbook Activities

27. Fill in the blanks.
28. Match the words.
29. Circle the correct answer.
30. Underline the verb.
31. Highlight the main idea.
32. Complete the sentence.
33. Choose the correct option.
34. Rearrange the words.
35. Write a short paragraph.
36. Summarize the passage.
37. Read the instructions carefully.
38. Follow the example.
39. Use the dictionary.
40. Find the meaning of this word.

Explaining and Guiding Tasks

41. This is how you do it.
42. First, read the question.
43. Then, think of the answer.
44. After that, write it down.
45. Finally, check your work.
46. Let me show you an example.
47. Please pay attention to the instructions.
48. Don't rush.
49. Take your time.
50. Ask me if you have doubts.

Checking Understanding

51. Do you understand?
52. Is that clear?
53. Any questions?
54. Can you repeat what I said?
55. Who can explain this?
56. What does this mean?

57. Can someone give another example?
58. Show me with your thumbs (up/down).
59. Let's go over it again.
60. Let me explain once more.

Reading and Writing

61. Read silently.
62. Read aloud.
63. Take turns reading.
64. Write in your notebooks.
65. Don't write yet.
66. Use complete sentences.
67. Write neatly.
68. Mind your spelling.
69. Edit your paragraph.
70. Check your grammar.
71. Use punctuation correctly.
72. Copy the notes from the board.
73. Write the heading.
74. Write today's date.
75. Make a list.
76. Write a dialogue.
77. Compose a short essay.
78. Create a story.
79. Fill out the worksheet.
80. Label the diagram.

Speaking and Listening

81. Speak clearly.
82. Speak loudly enough.
83. Don't interrupt.
84. Take turns speaking.
85. Listen to your partner.
86. Repeat after me.
87. Say it in English.
88. Ask your partner a question.
89. Answer in a full sentence.
90. Give your opinion.

91. Agree or disagree.
92. Describe the picture.
93. Tell a short story.
94. Make a presentation.
95. Role-play the dialogue.
96. Have a conversation.
97. Interview your partner.
98. Practice your pronunciation.
99. Use the new vocabulary.
100. Don't be shy, speak up.

Classroom Management
101. Be quiet, please.
102. No talking.
103. Raise your hand.
104. Wait your turn.
105. Don't shout.
106. Stay in your seat.
107. Keep your desk clean.
108. Don't chew gum.
109. Focus on your work.
110. Stop what you're doing.
111. Pay attention to the time.
112. Respect your classmates.
113. Be polite.
114. Don't copy.
115. Follow the rules.
116. Work quietly.
117. Keep your voice down.
118. Don't disturb others.
119. Help each other.
120. Stay on task.

Using the Board and Technology
121. Come to the board.
122. Write the answer on the board.
123. Use the marker.
124. Erase the board.

125. Watch the screen.
126. Listen to the audio.
127. Look at the slideshow.
128. Click on the link.
129. Open the app.
130. Log in to the website.
131. Type your answer.
132. Submit your work.
133. Share your screen.
134. Unmute yourself.
135. Turn on your camera.
136. Join the group chat.
137. Post your response.
138. Read the message.
139. Watch the video.
140. Pause the video.

Assessment and Review
141. Let's review.
142. Check your answers.
143. Let's correct it together.
144. How many did you get right?
145. Exchange papers.
146. Take a quiz.
147. It's time for a test.
148. Don't look at your friend's paper.
149. Try your best.
150. Submit your test.
151. We will grade it tomorrow.
152. Let's go over the answers.
153. Who got full marks?
154. Who needs help?
155. Let's do some revision.
156. Practice the exercises.
157. Review your notes.
158. Memorize the spelling.
159. Take notes while listening.
160. Recite the poem.

Ending the Class
161. Time is up.
162. Let's wrap up.
163. Any last questions?
164. Let's summarize.
165. What did we learn today?
166. Let's go over the main points.
167. Pack up your things.
168. Hand in your papers.
169. Clean up your desks.
170. Line up quietly.
171. Don't forget your homework.
172. Please be on time tomorrow.
173. Class dismissed.
174. Have a great day!
175. See you tomorrow.
176. Enjoy your break.
177. Stay safe.
178. Be ready for the quiz tomorrow.
179. Finish the rest at home.
180. You did a good job today.

Homework and Preparation
181. Write this down as homework.
182. Finish the worksheet.
183. Read the chapter.
184. Learn the new words.
185. Write the essay.
186. Prepare for the test.
187. Complete your assignment.
188. Bring your books tomorrow.
189. Don't forget to revise.
190. Submit your homework on time.
191. Get your parents to sign this.
192. Bring your dictionary.
193. Practice spelling.
194. Make flashcards.

195. Finish the story at home.
196. Record your voice reading.
197. Watch an English video.
198. Read aloud to your family.
199. Prepare a speech.
200. Come prepared.

Behavior and Social Conduct
201. Take your seat quickly.
202. Be mindful of others.
203. Take a deep breath and relax.
204. Read the board.
205. Keep your hands to yourself.
206. Be honest.
207. Think before you speak.
208. Respect different opinions.
209. Be enthusiastic.
210. Take notes.
211. Don't cross-talk.
212. Look at your textbook.
213. Organize your materials.
214. Finish on time.
215. Wait patiently.
216. Be a good listener.
217. Take care of your belongings.
218. Avoid distractions.
219. Join the discussion.
220. Raise your concern politely.
221. Share your ideas.
222. Stay engaged.
223. Monitor your progress.
224. Follow classroom routines.
225. Greet your classmates.
226. Greet your teacher.

Language Use and Skills
227. Give examples.
228. Clarify your doubts.

229. Ask for help if needed.
230. Paraphrase the sentence.
231. Listen without interrupting.
232. Use proper expressions.
233. Mind your tone.
234. Avoid slang in class.
235. Be punctual.
236. Stay focused.
237. Organize your notes.
238. Reflect on your learning.
239. Keep practicing.
240. Try again.
241. Don't give up.
242. Show your work.
243. Respect the time limits.
244. Clarify instructions.
245. Review your homework.
246. Look up new words.
247. Use new vocabulary in sentences.
248. Make corrections.
249. Acknowledge mistakes.
250. Try alternate solutions.

Advanced Skills and Analysis
251. Brainstorm ideas.
252. Skim the passage.
253. Scan for details.
254. Identify the topic.
255. Compare ideas.
256. Contrast points.
257. Find supporting details.
258. Check for coherence.
259. Re-read the sentence.
260. Correct the errors.
261. Proofread your work.
262. Write a conclusion.
263. Support your argument.
264. Organize your thoughts.

265. Create an outline.
266. Draft your essay.
267. Give a summary.
268. Add transitions.
269. Use connectors.
270. State your point.
271. Support with evidence.
272. Present your view.
273. Use quotations.
274. Mention the source.
275. Be original.
276. Avoid plagiarism.
277. Cite references.
278. Use paragraph structure.
279. Stick to the topic.
280. Stay within the word limit.
281. Use appropriate tense.
282. Use active voice.
283. Avoid repetition.
284. Vary your sentence structure.
285. Be concise.
286. Be clear.
287. Use appropriate vocabulary.
288. Use formal language.
289. Stay objective.
290. Use examples from real life.
291. Analyze the theme.
292. Explain the metaphor.
293. Interpret the poem.
294. Discuss the character.
295. Examine the plot.
296. Describe the setting.
297. Comment on the style.
298. Evaluate the text.
299. Provide feedback.
300. Be supportive.

Explaining Concepts

301. This means that...
302. In other words...
303. Let me simplify that.
304. It's like when...
305. Think of it as...
306. Another way to say this is...
307. What this shows is...
308. This is important because...
309. You can remember it by...
310. The rule here is...
311. We use this when...
312. This applies to...
313. Let me give you an example.
314. For instance...
315. Imagine you are...
316. Consider this situation...
317. You'll often see this in...
318. One key point is...
319. A common mistake is...
320. Don't confuse this with...
321. Here's how it works.
322. Let's break it down.
323. This part means...
324. Think of it step by step.
325. Look at this closely.
326. This connects with...
327. We can also say...
328. That's similar to...
329. That's different from...
330. You notice that...
331. This is known as...
332. We call this...
333. This kind of...
334. That's why we say...
335. Let me repeat it differently.
336. It helps to draw it out.
337. Look at this diagram.

338. Focus on this part.
339. Now compare it with...
340. Here's a trick to remember.
341. Here's a shortcut.
342. Let's underline the key words.
343. Now underline the verb.
344. The structure is...
345. This sentence pattern is...
346. That expression means...
347. In formal English, we say...
348. Informally, we might say...
349. Think about the context.
350. This is used in writing.
351. This is mostly spoken English.
352. The tense tells us...
353. The prefix means...
354. The suffix adds...
355. Let's revise this point.
356. You should also remember...
357. This is tricky, so watch closely.
358. Let's analyze this sentence.
359. What part of speech is this?
360. What function does this word have?
361. You can figure it out by...
362. We usually place this...
363. Notice the position of...
364. Why do you think that is?
365. Let's rephrase this.
366. Can we say this differently?
367. What's the opposite of this?
368. Let's think critically about this.
369. How would you explain this?
370. Try explaining it to a friend.
371. Let's explore the meaning.
372. This is an exception.
373. Be careful with this word.
374. This word has more than one meaning.
375. In this case, it means...

376. That reminds me of...
377. Let's highlight the difference.
378. This is similar but not the same.
379. Here's where it changes.
380. The tone here is...
381. The author wants to show...
382. What's the intention?
383. How does this affect meaning?
384. Let's connect this to what we learned before.
385. This builds on...
386. Let's summarize this idea.
387. Think of the main point.
388. What are the supporting details?
389. This helps us understand...
390. So what can we conclude?
391. Let's draw a conclusion.
392. The next step is...
393. This helps explain...
394. Remember this pattern.
395. Try applying this rule.
396. Let's take a closer look.
397. This ties in with...
398. That's the basic idea.
399. You'll need this for...
400. We'll come back to this later.

CHAPTER TWO

COMMON ERRORS

Common Errors (Wrong vs. Correct Sentences)

*Note: The following pairs include a common error (**Wrong**) made by teachers and its corrected version (**Correct**), along with the reason for the error.*

1. **Wrong:** She don't like coffee.
   Correct: She doesn't like coffee.
   Reason: Use **doesn't** with third person singular subjects.
2. **Wrong:** I didn't went to the party.
   Correct: I didn't go to the party.
   Reason: Use the **base verb** after **did** or **didn't**.
3. **Wrong:** He is my cousin brother.
   Correct: He is my cousin.
   Reason: The word **cousin** already implies the relationship; **brother** is redundant.
4. **Wrong:** She is more smarter than me.
   Correct: She is smarter than me.
   Reason: Do not use **more** with comparative adjectives like **smarter**.
5. **Wrong:** I am agree with you.
   Correct: I agree with you.
   Reason: **Agree** is a stative verb and is not used with **am**.
6. **Wrong:** He do his homework every day.
   Correct: He does his homework every day.
   Reason: Use **does** with third person singular subjects.
7. **Wrong:** She is liking the movie.
   Correct: She likes the movie.
   Reason: **Like** is a stative verb and is not used in the continuous form.

8. **Wrong:** My father is teacher.
   Correct: My father is a teacher.
   Reason: Use the article **a** before singular countable nouns.

9. **Wrong:** I have seen her yesterday.
   Correct: I saw her yesterday.
   Reason: Use **simple past** with time expressions like **yesterday.**

10. **Wrong:** He is working hardly.
    Correct: He is working hard.
    Reason: **Hardly** means "barely"; use **hard** for effort.

11. **Wrong:** I didn't knew the answer.
    Correct: I didn't know the answer.
    Reason: Use base verb after **didn't.**

12. **Wrong:** He don't has a pen.
    Correct: He doesn't have a pen.
    Reason: Use **doesn't have** for third person singular.

13. **Wrong:** Where you are going?
    Correct: Where are you going?
    Reason: Use correct word order in questions.

14. **Wrong:** I am hear a sound.
    Correct: I hear a sound.
    Reason: **Hear** is a stative verb and not used in continuous.

15. **Wrong:** She is more taller than him.
    Correct: She is taller than him.
    Reason: **More taller** is redundant.

16. **Wrong:** They goes to school daily.
    Correct: They go to school daily.
    Reason: Use **go** with plural subjects.

17. **Wrong:** He was died in the accident.
    Correct: He died in the accident.
    Reason: **Die** is not used in passive voice.

18. **Wrong:** My hairs are long.
    Correct: My hair is long.
    Reason: **Hair** is uncountable.

19. **Wrong:** She is my real sister.
    Correct: She is my sister.
    Reason: **Sister** already implies the relationship.

20. **Wrong:** He didn't came to class.
    Correct: He didn't come to class.

Reason: Use base verb after **didn't**.

21. **Wrong:** I didn't knew the answer.
    Correct: I didn't know the answer.
    Reason: Use base verb after **didn't**.

22. **Wrong:** He don't has a pen.
    Correct: He doesn't have a pen.
    Reason: Use **doesn't have** for third person singular.

23. **Wrong:** Where you are going?
    Correct: Where are you going?
    Reason: Use correct word order in questions.

24. **Wrong:** I am hear a sound.
    Correct: I hear a sound.
    Reason: **Hear** is a stative verb and not used in continuous.

25. **Wrong:** She is more taller than him.
    Correct: She is taller than him.
    Reason: **More taller** is redundant.

26. **Wrong:** They goes to school daily.
    Correct: They go to school daily.
    Reason: Use **go** with plural subjects.

27. **Wrong:** He was died in the accident.
    Correct: He died in the accident.
    Reason: **Die** is not used in passive voice.

28. **Wrong:** My hairs are long.
    Correct: My hair is long.
    Reason: **Hair** is uncountable.

29. **Wrong:** She is my real sister.
    Correct: She is my sister.
    Reason: **Sister** already implies the relationship.

30. **Wrong:** He didn't came to class.
    Correct: He didn't come to class.
    Reason: Use base verb after **didn't**.

31. **Wrong:** I didn't knew the answer.
    Correct: I didn't know the answer.
    Reason: Use base verb after **didn't**.

32. **Wrong:** He don't has a pen.
    Correct: He doesn't have a pen.
    Reason: Use **doesn't have** for third person singular.

33. **Wrong:** Where you are going?
    Correct: Where are you going?
    Reason: Use correct word order in questions.
34. **Wrong:** I am hear a sound.
    Correct: I hear a sound.
    Reason: Hear is a stative verb and not used in continuous.
35. **Wrong:** She is more taller than him.
    Correct: She is taller than him.
    Reason: More taller is redundant.
36. **Wrong:** They goes to school daily.
    Correct: They go to school daily.
    Reason: Use **go** with plural subjects.
37. **Wrong:** He was died in the accident.
    Correct: He died in the accident.
    Reason: Die is not used in passive voice.
38. **Wrong:** My hairs are long.
    Correct: My hair is long.
    Reason: Hair is uncountable.
39. **Wrong:** She is my real sister.
    Correct: She is my sister.
    Reason: Sister already implies the relationship.
40. **Wrong:** He didn't came to class.
    Correct: He didn't come to class.
    Reason: Use base verb after **didn't**.
41. **Wrong:** I am knowing the answer.
    Correct: I know the answer.
    Reason: Know is a stative verb and not used in the continuous form.
42. **Wrong:** She don't want to go.
    Correct: She doesn't want to go.
    Reason: Use **doesn't** for third person singular.
43. **Wrong:** He do not understand the lesson.
    Correct: He does not understand the lesson.
    Reason: Use **does** with third person singular subjects.
44. **Wrong:** They was happy.
    Correct: They were happy.
    Reason: Use **were** with plural subjects.
45. **Wrong:** The sceneries are beautiful.
    Correct: The scenery is beautiful.

Reason: Scenery is an uncountable noun.

46. **Wrong:** She said me the truth.
Correct: She told me the truth.
Reason: Say is not followed directly by an object.

47. **Wrong:** I am having two sisters.
Correct: I have two sisters.
Reason: Use **have** in simple present to show possession.

48. **Wrong:** The news are good.
Correct: The news is good.
Reason: News is uncountable and takes a singular verb.

49. **Wrong:** She is more better now.
Correct: She is better now.
Reason: Better is already a comparative form.

50. **Wrong:** The police is coming.
Correct: The police are coming.
Reason: Police is treated as a plural noun.

51. **Wrong:** I am going to abroad.
Correct: I am going abroad.
Reason: Abroad is an adverb and does not need a preposition.

52. **Wrong:** The teacher gave me an advice.
Correct: The teacher gave me a piece of advice.
Reason: Advice is uncountable.

53. **Wrong:** He is junior than me.
Correct: He is junior to me.
Reason: Use **to** after comparatives like **junior** and **senior**.

54. **Wrong:** She suggested me to read.
Correct: She suggested that I read.
Reason: Suggest is followed by a clause, not **object + to + verb**.

55. **Wrong:** I did a mistake.
Correct: I made a mistake.
Reason: We **make** mistakes, not **do** them.

56. **Wrong:** He is going to home.
Correct: He is going home.
Reason: Do not use **to** with **home**.

57. **Wrong:** She is waiting since two hours.
Correct: She has been waiting for two hours.
Reason: Use present perfect continuous with **since/for**.

58. **Wrong:** I am studying in this school since 2020.
    Correct: I have been studying in this school since 2020.
    Reason: Use **present perfect continuous** for actions continuing from the past.
59. **Wrong:** My friend he is a doctor.
    Correct: My friend is a doctor.
    Reason: Avoid **repeating the subject**.
60. **Wrong:** He told that he was tired.
    Correct: He said that he was tired.
    Reason: Use **said** when not followed by an object.
61. **Wrong:** I cannot able to go.
    Correct: I cannot go.
    Reason: **Can** already expresses ability; **able to** is redundant.
62. **Wrong:** He is good in English.
    Correct: He is good at English.
    Reason: Use the correct preposition **at**.
63. **Wrong:** I didn't took my lunch.
    Correct: I didn't take my lunch.
    Reason: Use base verb after **didn't**.
64. **Wrong:** She can to dance.
    Correct: She can dance.
    Reason: Do not use **to** after **can**.
65. **Wrong:** The class are noisy.
    Correct: The class is noisy.
    Reason: **Class** is a collective noun and takes singular verb.
66. **Wrong:** I am very much happy.
    Correct: I am very happy.
    Reason: Use **very** with adjectives, not **very much**.
67. **Wrong:** He is staying in hostel.
    Correct: He is staying in the hostel.
    Reason: Use **the** with singular countable nouns.
68. **Wrong:** She gave the exam well.
    Correct: She did well in the exam.
    Reason: Students **take** or **do well in** exams, not **give** them.
69. **Wrong:** I am suffering with fever.
    Correct: I have a fever.
    Reason: Use **have** for illnesses in English.

70. **Wrong:** He passed out from college.
    Correct: He graduated from college.
    Reason: Passed out means **fainted** in standard English.
71. **Wrong:** She is my cousin sister.
    Correct: She is my cousin.
    Reason: The word **cousin** already implies the relationship.
72. **Wrong:** They are going for a picnic.
    Correct: They are going on a picnic.
    Reason: The correct phrase is **on a picnic.**
73. **Wrong:** He is married with a doctor.
    Correct: He is married to a doctor.
    Reason: Use **to** with **married.**
74. **Wrong:** Let us to go outside.
    Correct: Let us go outside.
    Reason: Do not use **to** after **let.**
75. **Wrong:** I came to office by walk.
    Correct: I came to office on foot.
    Reason: Use **on foot**, not **by walk.**
76. **Wrong:** The teacher asked a doubt.
    Correct: The teacher asked a question.
    Reason: Use **question**, not **doubt**, in English.
77. **Wrong:** The team are winning.
    Correct: The team is winning.
    Reason: Use singular verb with **team.**
78. **Wrong:** I have seen him yesterday.
    Correct: I saw him yesterday.
    Reason: Use **simple past** with specific time.
79. **Wrong:** The teacher gave punishments.
    Correct: The teacher punished the students.
    Reason: Use **punish** as a verb.
80. **Wrong:** She is more prettier.
    Correct: She is prettier.
    Reason: Do not use **more** with comparatives.
81. **Wrong:** The news are shocking.
    Correct: The news is shocking.
    Reason: News is uncountable.
82. **Wrong:** I did not knew that.
    Correct: I did not know that.

Reason: Use base verb after **did not**.

83. **Wrong:** He is in leave.
    Correct: He is on leave.
    Reason: The correct phrase is **on leave**.

84. **Wrong:** I am going to shopping.
    Correct: I am going shopping.
    Reason: Do not use **to** with **go shopping**.

85. **Wrong:** She told me that to wait.
    Correct: She told me to wait.
    Reason: Remove **that** before infinitive.

86. **Wrong:** He is the most smartest student.
    Correct: He is the smartest student.
    Reason: Do not use **most** with superlatives.

87. **Wrong:** She is elder than me.
    Correct: She is older than me.
    Reason: Use **older** for general comparisons.

88. **Wrong:** He is going to outside.
    Correct: He is going outside.
    Reason: Do not use **to** with adverbs like **outside**.

89. **Wrong:** I have a good news.
    Correct: I have some good news.
    Reason: **News** is uncountable.

90. **Wrong:** I am understanding the topic.
    Correct: I understand the topic.
    Reason: **Understand** is a stative verb.

91. **Wrong:** She is not coming school today.
    Correct: She is not coming to school today.
    Reason: Use **to** before **school**.

92. **Wrong:** I am watch TV.
    Correct: I am watching TV.
    Reason: Use correct **continuous tense**.

93. **Wrong:** She not came to class.
    Correct: She didn't come to class.
    Reason: Use **didn't** for negative past tense.

94. **Wrong:** The milk are boiling.
    Correct: The milk is boiling.
    Reason: **Milk** is uncountable and singular.

95. **Wrong:** The clock is in the wall.
    Correct: The clock is on the wall.
    Reason: Use the correct preposition **on**

96. **Wrong:** I didn't knew she was here.
    Correct: I didn't know she was here.
    Reason: Use the **base verb** after **didn't**.

97. **Wrong:** He is more happier now.
    Correct: He is happier now.
    Reason: Don't use **more** with comparatives

98. **Wrong:** We went for shopping.
    Correct: We went shopping.
    Reason: Go shopping doesn't take **for**

99. **Wrong:** He gave me an advice.
    Correct: He gave me some advice.
    Reason: Advice is uncountable and doesn't use **an.**

100. **Wrong:** The girl which is singing is my sister.
     Correct: The girl who is singing is my sister.
     Reason: Use **who** for people.

101. **Wrong:** I met with her yesterday.
     Correct: I met her yesterday.
     Reason: Drop **with** after **meet.**

102. **Wrong:** She is my cousin sister.
     Correct: She is my cousin.
     Reason: Cousin already shows the relation.

103. **Wrong:** The house is made by bricks.
     Correct: The house is made of bricks.
     Reason: Use **of** with materials.

104. **Wrong:** He is more fast than his brother.
     Correct: He is faster than his brother.
     Reason: Use the comparative form **faster** directly.

105. **Wrong:** I returned back home.
     Correct: I returned home.
     Reason: Return already implies **back.**

106. **Wrong:** He explained me the topic.
     Correct: He explained the topic to me.
     Reason: Use **to** when the object follows the thing explained.

107. **Wrong:** He is the most fastest runner.
     Correct: He is the fastest runner.

Reason: Don't use **most** with superlatives.

108. **Wrong:** I have many works to do.

     Correct: I have much work to do.

     Reason: Work is uncountable.

109. **Wrong:** He came to office by walk.

     Correct: He came to office on foot.

     Reason: The correct expression is **on foot**.

110. **Wrong:** The child was died.

     Correct: The child died.

     Reason: Die is an intransitive verb and not used in passive form.

111. **Wrong:** I didn't attended the class.

     Correct: I didn't attend the class.

     Reason: Use base form after **didn't**.

112. **Wrong:** He suggested me to apply.

     Correct: He suggested that I apply.

     Reason: Suggest takes a clause, not object + infinitive.

113. **Wrong:** He is addicted in drugs.

     Correct: He is addicted to drugs.

     Reason: Use **to** after **addicted**.

114. **Wrong:** The house comprises of five rooms.

     Correct: The house comprises five rooms.

     Reason: Don't use **of** after **comprises**.

115. **Wrong:** I didn't used to smoke.

     Correct: I didn't use to smoke.

     Reason: After **didn't**, use base verb **use**.

116. **Wrong:** I am late than you.

     Correct: I am later than you.

     Reason: Use **later** for comparisons.

117. **Wrong:** She is best in the class.

     Correct: She is the best in the class.

     Reason: Use **the** with superlative adjectives.

118. **Wrong:** He is working in Infosys Company.

     Correct: He is working in Infosys.

     Reason: Don't add **Company** after a company's name.

119. **Wrong:** He is in good mood.

     Correct: He is in a good mood.

     Reason: Use **a** before singular countable nouns.

120. **Wrong:** She told to me the truth.
Correct: She told me the truth.
Reason: Don't use **to** with **told** when the object follows.

121. **Wrong:** The scenery is beautifuls.
Correct: The scenery is beautiful.
Reason: **Scenery** is uncountable and singular.

122. **Wrong:** This is a very unique idea.
Correct: This is a unique idea.
Reason: **Unique** means one of a kind; don't modify with **very**.

123. **Wrong:** He is more senior than me.
Correct: He is senior to me.
Reason: Use **to** with **senior**, not **than**

124. **Wrong:** She went to abroad.
Correct: She went abroad.
Reason: Don't use **to** before **abroad**.

125. **Wrong:** I have returned back the book.
Correct: I have returned the book.
Reason: **Return** implies **back** already.

126. **Wrong:** She discussed about the issue.
Correct: She discussed the issue.
Reason: **Discuss** doesn't take **about**.

127. **Wrong:** The room is lacking of light.
Correct: The room lacks light.
Reason: Use **lack** as a transitive verb.

128. **Wrong:** He is not listening me.
Correct: He is not listening to me.
Reason: Use **to** with **listen**.

129. **Wrong:** The building consists with ten floors.
Correct: The building consists of ten floors.
Reason: Use **of** with **consists**

130. **Wrong:** He was very angry on me.
Correct: He was very angry with me.
Reason: Use **angry with**, not **angry on**.

131. **Wrong:** I met him before two days.
Correct: I met him two days ago.
Reason: Use **ago** with time references, not **before**.

132. **Wrong:** He entered into the room.
Correct: He entered the room.

Reason: Enter doesn't need **into**.

133. **Wrong:** She is good in dancing.
Correct: She is good at dancing.
Reason: Use **at** with **good** for skills.

134. **Wrong:** He insisted me to go.
Correct: He insisted that I go.
Reason: Insist is followed by a clause, not object + infinitive.

135. **Wrong:** I replied him.
Correct: I replied to him.
Reason: Use **to** after **reply**.

136. **Wrong:** She was died last week.
Correct: She died last week.
Reason: Die is not used in passive.

137. **Wrong:** She described me the scene.
Correct: She described the scene to me.
Reason: Use **to** when the indirect object follows.

138. **Wrong:** He is afraid from dogs.
Correct: He is afraid of dogs.
Reason: Use **of** with **afraid**.

139. **Wrong:** The room is full with people.
Correct: The room is full of people.
Reason: Use **full of**, not **full with**.

140. **Wrong:** She resembles with her mother.
Correct: She resembles her mother.
Reason: Resemble does not take **with**.

141. **Wrong:** I prefer tea than coffee.
Correct: I prefer tea to coffee.
Reason: Use **to** with **prefer**.

142. **Wrong:** He married with a French woman.
Correct: He married a French woman.
Reason: Don't use **with** after **married** in active voice.

143. **Wrong:** The cost of the house is too much high.
Correct: The cost of the house is very high.
Reason: Use **very** with adjectives, not **too much**

144. **Wrong:** I am living here from five years.
Correct: I have been living here for five years.
Reason: Use **present perfect continuous** with **for/from** time.

145. **Wrong:** I didn't wrote the message.
Correct: I didn't write the message.
Reason: Use the base verb after **didn't**.

146. **Wrong:** He is one of the best player.
Correct: He is one of the best players.
Reason: Use plural noun after **one of the**.

147. **Wrong:** She told that she is busy.
Correct: She said that she is busy.
Reason: Use **said** unless followed by an object.

148. **Wrong:** They enjoyed during the picnic.
Correct: They enjoyed the picnic.
Reason: Avoid redundant use of **during** after **enjoyed**.

149. **Wrong:** The road is very much long.
Correct: The road is very long.
Reason: Use **very**, not **very much**, with adjectives.

150. **Wrong:** She is superior than him.
Correct: She is superior to him.
Reason: Use **to** with **superior**.

151. **Wrong:** I am suffering from fever.
Correct: I have a fever.
Reason: Use **have** for illness in English.

152. **Wrong:** He is more richer than me.
Correct: He is richer than me.
Reason: Do not use **more** with comparatives.

153. **Wrong:** They discussed about the topic.
Correct: They discussed the topic.
Reason: **Discuss** should not be followed by **about**.

154. **Wrong:** I saw a dream last night.
Correct: I had a dream last night.
Reason: The correct phrase is **had a dream**.

155. **Wrong:** The sceneries are amazing.
Correct: The scenery is amazing.
Reason: **Scenery** is uncountable.

156. **Wrong:** He was born on 1995.
Correct: He was born in 1995.
Reason: Use **in** with years.

157. **Wrong:** She is the most tallest girl.
Correct: She is the tallest girl.

Reason: Don't use **most** with superlatives.

158. **Wrong:** I have visited to the museum.
Correct: I have visited the museum.
Reason: Do not use **to** after **visited**.

159. **Wrong:** She is more kinder than her sister.
Correct: She is kinder than her sister.
Reason: More kinder is incorrect.

160. **Wrong:** My all friends are here.
Correct: All my friends are here.
Reason: Use **all my friends**, not **my all friends**.

161. **Wrong:** He is my cousin brother.
Correct: He is my cousin.
Reason: Cousin already indicates the relationship.

162. **Wrong:** He returned back the pen.
Correct: He returned the pen.
Reason: Back is redundant after **returned**.

163. **Wrong:** She married with a doctor.
Correct: She married a doctor.
Reason: Don't use **with** after **married** in active voice.

164. **Wrong:** He does not knows the answer.
Correct: He does not know the answer.
Reason: Use the base verb after **does not**.

165. **Wrong:** He did a mistake.
Correct: He made a mistake.
Reason: We **make** mistakes, not **do** them.

166. **Wrong:** She is waiting here since two hours.
Correct: She has been waiting here for two hours.
Reason: Use present perfect continuous with **for/since**.

167. **Wrong:** I am having a headache.
Correct: I have a headache.
Reason: Use **have** for illness or possession.

168. **Wrong:** She is my bestest friend.
Correct: She is my best friend.
Reason: Bestest is not a valid word.

169. **Wrong:** He is the eldest in the team.
Correct: He is the oldest in the team.
Reason: Use **oldest** for general comparisons.

170. **Wrong:** Let us to go now.
     Correct: Let us go now.
     Reason: Do not use **to** after **let**.
171. **Wrong:** He is going to school by walk.
     Correct: He is going to school on foot.
     Reason: The correct phrase is **on foot**.
172. **Wrong:** He is sitting in the table.
     Correct: He is sitting at the table.
     Reason: Use **at** with **table**.
173. **Wrong:** The news are good.
     Correct: The news is good.
     Reason: **News** is uncountable and singular.
174. **Wrong:** She is junior than me.
     Correct: She is junior to me.
     Reason: Use **to** with **junior**.
175. **Wrong:** She came to home late.
     Correct: She came home late.
     Reason: Do not use **to** before **home**.
176. **Wrong:** She sang good in the competition.
     Correct: She sang well in the competition.
     Reason: Use **well** to describe actions
177. **Wrong:** He is working hardly.
     Correct: He is working hard.
     Reason: **Hardly** means **barely**, not **with effort**.
178. **Wrong:** She has many furnitures.
     Correct: She has much furniture.
     Reason: **Furniture** is uncountable.
179. **Wrong:** He said me to come.
     Correct: He told me to come.
     Reason: **Tell** is used with an indirect object.
180. **Wrong:** We can able to solve it.
     Correct: We can solve it.
     Reason: **Can** already shows ability; **able to** is redundant.
181. **Wrong:** The teacher gave me an information.
     Correct: The teacher gave me some information.
     Reason: **Information** is uncountable.
182. **Wrong:** She is sitting beside me.
     Correct: She is sitting next to me.

Reason: Next to is more common in modern usage.

183. **Wrong:** I have seen her yesterday.
Correct: I saw her yesterday.
Reason: Use **simple past** with specific time references.

184. **Wrong:** He is a honest man.
Correct: He is an honest man.
Reason: Use **an** before vowel sounds.

185. **Wrong:** I and my friend went to the store.
Correct: My friend and I went to the store.
Reason: Put the other person before **I** in compound subjects.

186. **Wrong:** The baby cried because it was hunger.
Correct: The baby cried because it was hungry.
Reason: Use adjective **hungry**, not noun **hunger.**

187. **Wrong:** He is more strong than his brother.
Correct: He is stronger than his brother.
Reason: Don't use **more** with comparatives.

188. **Wrong:** I am waiting here since morning.
Correct: I have been waiting here since morning.
Reason: Use **present perfect continuous** with **since.**

189. **Wrong:** She is more intelligent than any girl in the class.
Correct: She is more intelligent than any other girl in the class.
Reason: Use **any other** to exclude the subject.

190. **Wrong:** I am not understanding this.
Correct: I don't understand this.
Reason: Understand is a stative verb, not used in continuous form.

191. **Wrong:** The students were late because the traffic.
Correct: The students were late because of the traffic.
Reason: Use **because of** + noun.

192. **Wrong:** He is more better than before.
Correct: He is better than before.
Reason: More better is incorrect; use just **better.**

193. **Wrong:** She said me that she was tired.
Correct: She told me that she was tired.
Reason: Say is not followed by an object without **to.**

194. **Wrong:** The clock is in the wall.
Correct: The clock is on the wall.
Reason: Use correct preposition **on** for surfaces.

195. **Wrong:** She asked to me a question.
Correct: She asked me a question.
Reason: Do not use **to** after **ask** when an indirect object is used.

196. **Wrong:** He is married with a dentist.
Correct: He is married to a dentist.
Reason: Use **to** with **married**.

197. **Wrong:** I go always to the gym.
Correct: I always go to the gym.
Reason: Place frequency adverbs before the main verb.

198. **Wrong:** She can able to drive.
Correct: She can drive.
Reason: Do not use **can** and **able to** together.

199. **Wrong:** It is raining since morning.
Correct: It has been raining since morning.
Reason: Use present perfect continuous for actions from the past until now.

200. **Wrong:** He is good in math.
Correct: He is good at math.
Reason: Use **at** with **good** for subjects or skills.

201. **Wrong:** I suggested him to rest.
Correct: I suggested that he rest.
Reason: **Suggest** should be followed by a clause, not object + infinitive.

202. **Wrong:** The teacher gave me many homeworks.
Correct: The teacher gave me much homework.
Reason: **Homework** is uncountable.

203. **Wrong:** She said me the story.
Correct: She told me the story.
Reason: Use **tell** with an object; **say** does not take an object directly.

204. **Wrong:** The team are playing well.
Correct: The team is playing well.
Reason: Use singular verb with collective nouns when treated as one unit.

205. **Wrong:** I am here since January.
Correct: I have been here since January.
Reason: Use present perfect continuous for ongoing states.

206. **Wrong:** He discussed about the plan.
Correct: He discussed the plan.
Reason: **Discuss** is not followed by **about**.

207. **Wrong:** She is suffering from cough.
Correct: She has a cough.
Reason: Use **have** to describe medical conditions.

208. **Wrong:** I did not knew that.
Correct: I did not know that.
Reason: Use the base verb after **did**.

209. **Wrong:** She is more braver than him.
Correct: She is braver than him.
Reason: Do not use **more** with comparatives.

210. **Wrong:** My brother he is a doctor.
Correct: My brother is a doctor.
Reason: Avoid repetition of the subject

211. **Wrong:** This house is built by bricks.
Correct: This house is built of bricks.
Reason: Use **of** with materials.

212. **Wrong:** I prefer coffee than tea.
Correct: I prefer coffee to tea.
Reason: Use **to** with **prefer**.

213. **Wrong:** He replied me rudely.
Correct: He replied to me rudely.
Reason: Use **to** after **reply**.

214. **Wrong:** She is listening music.
Correct: She is listening to music.
Reason: Use **to** with **listen**.

215. **Wrong:** He resembles with his father.
Correct: He resembles his father.
Reason: Do not use **with** after **resemble**.

216. **Wrong:** Let's go for shopping.
Correct: Let's go shopping.
Reason: Do not use **for** with **go shopping**.

217. **Wrong:** I have seen him yesterday.
Correct: I saw him yesterday.
Reason: Use **simple past** with specific time references.

218. **Wrong:** He is best player in the team.
Correct: He is the best player in the team.
Reason: Use **the** with superlatives.

219. **Wrong:** She didn't went to school.
Correct: She didn't go to school.

Reason: Use the base verb after **didn't**.

220. **Wrong:** I look forward to meet you.
Correct: I look forward to meeting you.
Reason: Look forward to should be followed by a **gerund**.

221. **Wrong:** She enjoys to dance.
Correct: She enjoys dancing.
Reason: Enjoy is followed by a **gerund**.

222. **Wrong:** He is angry on me.
Correct: He is angry with me.
Reason: Use **angry with**, not **angry on**.

223. **Wrong:** He is capable to solve it.
Correct: He is capable of solving it.
Reason: Use **capable of** + gerund.

224. **Wrong:** This is more preferable.
Correct: This is preferable.
Reason: Preferable already implies comparison.

225. **Wrong:** We discussed about the issue yesterday.
Correct: We discussed the issue yesterday.
Reason: Do not use **about** with **discuss**.

226. **Wrong:** He denied to go.
Correct: He denied going.
Reason: Deny is followed by a **gerund**.

227. **Wrong:** They left from the room.
Correct: They left the room.
Reason: Do not use **from** after **left**.

228. **Wrong:** She told that she is coming.
Correct: She said that she is coming.
Reason: Use **said** unless followed by an object.

229. **Wrong:** He availed the opportunity.
Correct: He availed himself of the opportunity.
Reason: Use the reflexive form with **avail**.

230. **Wrong:** She is my cousin sister.
Correct: She is my cousin.
Reason: Cousin alone is sufficient.

231. **Wrong:** This plan is more better.
Correct: This plan is better.
Reason: Avoid double comparatives.

232. **Wrong:** I asked to him a question.
     Correct: I asked him a question.
     Reason: Remove **to** when an object directly follows.
233. **Wrong:** I didn't knew the answer.
     Correct: I didn't know the answer.
     Reason: Use base form after **didn't**.
234. **Wrong:** She is elder to me.
     Correct: She is older than me.
     Reason: Use **older** for general comparisons.
235. **Wrong:** She is very much talented.
     Correct: She is very talented.
     Reason: Use **very**, not **very much**, with adjectives.
236. **Wrong:** I doubt if he will come.
     Correct: I wonder if he will come.
     Reason: Use **wonder** instead of **doubt** in this context.
237. **Wrong:** I have no any problem.
     Correct: I have no problem.
     Reason: Do not use **no** and **any** together.
238. **Wrong:** He is more taller than me.
     Correct: He is taller than me.
     Reason: Avoid double comparatives.
239. **Wrong:** I reached to the station.
     Correct: I reached the station.
     Reason: Do not use **to** with **reached**.
240. **Wrong:** This is the most perfect design.
     Correct: This is the perfect design.
     Reason: **Perfect** is absolute; don't use **most** with it.
241. **Wrong:** The baby cried due to hunger.
     Correct: The baby cried because of hunger.
     Reason: Use **because of** to explain reasons.
242. **Wrong:** He is my cousin brother.
     Correct: He is my cousin.
     Reason: Use only **cousin**; **brother** is redundant.
243. **Wrong:** She was born at 1998.
     Correct: She was born in 1998.
     Reason: Use **in** with years.
244. **Wrong:** The program starts on 6 PM.
     Correct: The program starts at 6 PM.

Reason: Use **at** with clock time.

245. **Wrong:** He is going to abroad.
Correct: He is going abroad.
Reason: Abroad is an adverb and does not take **to**

246. **Wrong:** She is living here since 5 years.
Correct: She has been living here for 5 years.
Reason: Use present perfect continuous with **for/since**.

247. **Wrong:** He is lacking in confidence.
Correct: He lacks confidence.
Reason: Use **lack** as a transitive verb.

248. **Wrong:** I have seen her two days before.
Correct: I saw her two days ago.
Reason: Use **ago** with time references.

249. **Wrong:** He entered into the room silently.
Correct: He entered the room silently.
Reason: Enter does not take **into**.

250. **Wrong:** The book consists with five chapters.
Correct: The book consists of five chapters.
Reason: Use **of** with **consists**.

251. **Wrong:** I explained him the problem.
Correct: I explained the problem to him.
Reason: Use **to** when the object follows the thing explained.

252. **Wrong:** The scenery of Kashmir are beautiful.
Correct: The scenery of Kashmir is beautiful.
Reason: Scenery is uncountable and takes a singular verb.

253. **Wrong:** I demand for an explanation.
Correct: I demand an explanation.
Reason: Do not use **for** after **demand**.

254. **Wrong:** I went to my home.
Correct: I went home.
Reason: Do not use **to** before **home**.

255. **Wrong:** She is senior than me.
Correct: She is senior to me.
Reason: Use **to** with **senior**.

256. **Wrong:** He is capable to do it.
Correct: He is capable of doing it.
Reason: Use **of + gerund** with **capable**.

257. **Wrong:** He insisted to go.
     Correct: He insisted on going.
     Reason: Use **on + gerund** with **insist**.

258. **Wrong:** He was died last year.
     Correct: He died last year.
     Reason: **Die** is intransitive and not used in the passive voice.

259. **Wrong:** She is afraid from dogs.
     Correct: She is afraid of dogs.
     Reason: Use **of** with **afraid**.

260. **Wrong:** She did a blunder.
     Correct: She made a blunder.
     Reason: We **make** blunders, not **do** them.

261. **Wrong:** He delivered a good speech in the function.
     Correct: He gave a good speech at the function.
     Reason: Use **give** for **speech** and **at** for events.

262. **Wrong:** The bird flew in the sky.
     Correct: The bird flew into the sky.
     Reason: Use **into** for motion towards a space.

263. **Wrong:** She is habitual of smoking.
     Correct: She is habituated to smoking.
     Reason: Use **habituated to** with gerund.

264. **Wrong:** He was agreed with the decision.
     Correct: He agreed with the decision.
     Reason: **Agree** is not used in the passive voice.

265. **Wrong:** She resembles to her mother.
     Correct: She resembles her mother.
     Reason: Do not use **to** with **resemble**.

266. **Wrong:** The criminal was hung yesterday.
     Correct: The criminal was hanged yesterday.
     Reason: Use **hanged** for execution.

267. **Wrong:** I have completed my studies in 2020.
     Correct: I completed my studies in 2020.
     Reason: Use **simple past** with a specific time.

268. **Wrong:** He went to picnic with friends.
     Correct: He went on a picnic with friends.
     Reason: Use **on a picnic**, not **to picnic**.

269. **Wrong:** I gave an examination last week.
     Correct: I took an examination last week.

Reason: Use **take an exam**, not **give**.

270. **Wrong:** My house is near to the station.
Correct: My house is near the station.
Reason: Do not use **to** after **near**.

271. **Wrong:** He explained me about the topic.
Correct: He explained the topic to me.
Reason: Do not use **about** with **explain**.

272. **Wrong:** She said me to leave.
Correct: She told me to leave.
Reason: Use **tell** + object + to + verb.

273. **Wrong:** He is ill from Monday.
Correct: He has been ill since Monday.
Reason: Use **present perfect continuous** with **since**.

274. **Wrong:** He was born at 2001.
Correct: He was born in 2001.
Reason: Use **in** with years.

275. **Wrong:** He is in the school.
Correct: He is at school.
Reason: Use **at** for general location at school.

276. **Wrong:** He took admission in the college.
Correct: He got admission to the college.
Reason: Use **got admission to**, not **took**.

277. **Wrong:** I went in the room.
Correct: I went into the room.
Reason: Use **into** for movement.

278. **Wrong:** The baby was sleeping when I have come.
Correct: The baby was sleeping when I came.
Reason: Use **simple past** after **past continuous**.

279. **Wrong:** I met John before two days.
Correct: I met John two days ago.
Reason: Use **ago**, not **before**.

280. **Wrong:** She went in USA last year.
Correct: She went to the USA last year.
Reason: Use **to the USA**.

281. **Wrong:** He committed a mistake.
Correct: He made a mistake.
Reason: Use **make a mistake**.

282. **Wrong:** She returned back from office.
Correct: She returned from office.
Reason: Back is redundant after **returned**.

283. **Wrong:** The manager is in leave.
Correct: The manager is on leave.
Reason: Use **on leave**.

284. **Wrong:** He has been died.
Correct: He has died.
Reason: Die is not used in the passive voice.

285. **Wrong:** He is lacking of discipline.
Correct: He lacks discipline.
Reason: Use **lack** as a transitive verb.

286. **Wrong:** She is more senior than me.
Correct: She is senior to me.
Reason: Do not use **more** with **senior**.

287. **Wrong:** We discussed about politics.
Correct: We discussed politics.
Reason: Do not use **about** with **discuss**.

288. **Wrong:** The student was appeared in the exam.
Correct: The student appeared in the exam.
Reason: Appear is not used in the passive voice.

289. **Wrong:** He goes to office by walk.
Correct: He goes to office on foot.
Reason: Use **on foot**, not **by walk**.

290. **Wrong:** I didn't went to the market.
Correct: I didn't go to the market.
Reason: Use base verb after **didn't**.

291. **Wrong:** She gave me a good advice.
Correct: She gave me some good advice.
Reason: Advice is uncountable.

292. **Wrong:** He denied to accept the offer.
Correct: He denied accepting the offer.
Reason: Use a **gerund** after **deny**.

293. **Wrong:** He was playing good.
Correct: He was playing well.
Reason: Use **well** for actions, not **good**.

294. **Wrong:** He returned back to his village.
Correct: He returned to his village.

Reason: Back is unnecessary with **returned.**

295. **Wrong:** She married with a teacher.
Correct: She married a teacher.
Reason: Do not use **with** after **married** in active voice.

296. **Wrong:** The students are in the class.
Correct: The students are in class.
Reason: Use **in class** to mean attending a session.

297. **Wrong:** He entered into the office.
Correct: He entered the office.
Reason: Enter does not require **into.**

298. **Wrong:** We enjoyed in the party.
Correct: We enjoyed the party.
Reason: Do not use **in** after **enjoyed.**

299. **Wrong:** She is very much beautiful.
Correct: She is very beautiful.
Reason: Use **very** instead of **very much** with adjectives.

300. **Wrong:** They left from the station.
Correct: They left the station.
Reason: Leave does not take **from.**

301. **Wrong:** I met with her yesterday.
Correct: I met her yesterday.
Reason: Do not use **with** after **met.**

302. **Wrong:** He did not wrote the exam.
Correct: He did not write the exam.
Reason: Use base verb after **did.**

303. **Wrong:** The scenery are beautiful.
Correct: The scenery is beautiful.
Reason: Scenery is uncountable and singular.

304. **Wrong:** He is going to his home.
Correct: He is going home.
Reason: Do not use **to** with **home.**

305. **Wrong:** This place is more preferable.
Correct: This place is preferable.
Reason: Preferable does not need **more.**

306. **Wrong:** The train is arrived.
Correct: The train has arrived.
Reason: Use **present perfect** for recent events.

307. **Wrong:** I know to swim.
Correct: I know how to swim.
Reason: Use **how to** after **know** for expressing skills.

308. **Wrong:** I returned back the book.
Correct: I returned the book.
Reason: Back is redundant with **returned**.

309. **Wrong:** He speaks English good.
Correct: He speaks English well.
Reason: Use **well** to describe an action.

310. **Wrong:** She asked that what was the matter.
Correct: She asked what the matter was.
Reason: Avoid redundant **that** in indirect questions.

311. **Wrong:** He is taller from his brother.
Correct: He is taller than his brother.
Reason: Use **than** in comparisons.

312. **Wrong:** She is more intelligent from all.
Correct: She is more intelligent than all others.
Reason: Use **than all others** in comparisons.

313. **Wrong:** The teacher gave me an information.
Correct: The teacher gave me some information.
Reason: Information is uncountable.

314. **Wrong:** He is waiting since an hour.
Correct: He has been waiting for an hour.
Reason: Use **present perfect continuous** with **for**.

315. **Wrong:** The man is blind from one eye.
Correct: The man is blind in one eye.
Reason: Use **in** with body parts.

316. **Wrong:** She explained me the process.
Correct: She explained the process to me.
Reason: Use **to** when the object comes after.

317. **Wrong:** I suggested him a solution.
Correct: I suggested a solution to him.
Reason: Suggest requires **to** before the indirect object.

318. **Wrong:** She insisted me to go.
Correct: She insisted that I go.
Reason: Insist is followed by a clause, not object + infinitive.

319. **Wrong:** He was playing bad.
Correct: He was playing badly.

Reason: Use **badly** to describe actions.

320. **Wrong:** I request you to kindly help me.
     Correct: I kindly request you to help me.
     Reason: Avoid redundant politeness expressions.

321. **Wrong:** She is very much tired.
     Correct: She is very tired.
     Reason: Use **very** with adjectives, not **very much**.

322. **Wrong:** They are discussing about the issue.
     Correct: They are discussing the issue.
     Reason: Do not use **about** with **discuss**.

323. **Wrong:** The reason of his failure is because he was careless.
     Correct: The reason for his failure is that he was careless.
     Reason: Do not use **reason...because** together.

324. **Wrong:** She fell down and was unconscious.
     Correct: She fell down and became unconscious.
     Reason: Use **became** to indicate state change.

325. **Wrong:** He is my cousin brother.
     Correct: He is my cousin.
     Reason: **Cousin** already implies the relationship.

326. **Wrong:** I met him in last week.
     Correct: I met him last week.
     Reason: Do not use **in** before time expressions like **last week**.

327. **Wrong:** This chair is made by wood.
     Correct: This chair is made of wood.
     Reason: Use **of** to show material.

328. **Wrong:** He was running fastly.
     Correct: He was running fast.
     Reason: **Fast** is both an adjective and an adverb.

329. **Wrong:** I went to shopping.
     Correct: I went shopping.
     Reason: Do not use **to** before **shopping** with **go**.

330. **Wrong:** She is more better than him.
     Correct: She is better than him.
     Reason: Do not use **more** with comparatives.

331. **Wrong:** They enjoyed at the party.
     Correct: They enjoyed the party.
     Reason: **Enjoy** is a transitive verb.

332. **Wrong:** I took my breakfast.
     Correct: I had my breakfast.
     Reason: Use **had** with meals.
333. **Wrong:** She is afraid from spiders.
     Correct: She is afraid of spiders.
     Reason: Use **of** with **afraid**.
334. **Wrong:** He was angry on me.
     Correct: He was angry with me.
     Reason: Use **angry with**, not **on**.
335. **Wrong:** She was born at 1999.
     Correct: She was born in 1999.
     Reason: Use **in** with years.
336. **Wrong:** I came to office by foot.
     Correct: I came to office on foot.
     Reason: Use **on foot** for walking.
337. **Wrong:** She is good in math.
     Correct: She is good at math.
     Reason: Use **at** with subjects and skills.
338. **Wrong:** He denied to come.
     Correct: He denied coming.
     Reason: Use **gerund** after **deny**.
339. **Wrong:** The child is lacking in manners.
     Correct: The child lacks manners.
     Reason: Use **lack** as a transitive verb.
340. **Wrong:** I am waiting since two hours.
     Correct: I have been waiting for two hours.
     Reason: Use **present perfect continuous** with **for/since**.
341. **Wrong:** He does not knows the answer.
     Correct: He does not know the answer.
     Reason: Use base form after **does not**.
342. **Wrong:** She explained me about the accident.
     Correct: She explained the accident to me.
     Reason: Do not use **about** with **explain**; use **to** for the person.
343. **Wrong:** He said to me to wait.
     Correct: He told me to wait.
     Reason: Use **told** + object + infinitive.
344. **Wrong:** She is liking the weather.
     Correct: She likes the weather.

Reason: Like is a stative verb; do not use in continuous tense.

345. **Wrong:** I have no any idea.
Correct: I have no idea.
Reason: Do not use **no** and **any** together.

346. **Wrong:** She is my cousin sister.
Correct: She is my cousin.
Reason: Cousin already shows the relation.

347. **Wrong:** He is in the home.
Correct: He is at home.
Reason: Use **at home**, not **in the home**.

348. **Wrong:** They are in the school.
Correct: They are at school.
Reason: Use **at school** for location.

349. **Wrong:** She has a good knowledge.
Correct: She has good knowledge.
Reason: Knowledge is uncountable.

350. **Wrong:** I am knowing the answer.
Correct: I know the answer.
Reason: Know is a stative verb.

351. **Wrong:** We went for shopping yesterday.
Correct: We went shopping yesterday.
Reason: Do not use **for** with **go shopping**.

352. **Wrong:** He is working hardly.
Correct: He is working hard.
Reason: Hardly means **barely**; use **hard**.

353. **Wrong:** The news are good.
Correct: The news is good.
Reason: News is uncountable and singular.

354. **Wrong:** He is senior than me.
Correct: He is senior to me.
Reason: Use **to** with **senior**.

355. **Wrong:** This is the more important point.
Correct: This is the most important point.
Reason: Use superlative **most** for comparisons.

356. **Wrong:** The sceneries here are beautiful.
Correct: The scenery here is beautiful.
Reason: Scenery is uncountable.

357. **Wrong:** He is my real brother.
Correct: He is my brother.
Reason: Brother already implies blood relation.

358. **Wrong:** I returned back from work.
Correct: I returned from work.
Reason: Back is redundant.

359. **Wrong:** She is good in cooking.
Correct: She is good at cooking.
Reason: Use **at** with **good**.

360. **Wrong:** He was born on 2000.
Correct: He was born in 2000.
Reason: Use **in** with years.

361. **Wrong:** He has completed his graduation.
Correct: He has graduated.
Reason: Graduated is the correct usage.

362. **Wrong:** The students gave the exam.
Correct: The students took the exam.
Reason: Use **take an exam.**

363. **Wrong:** She told that she was busy.
Correct: She said that she was busy.
Reason: Use **said** unless followed by an object.

364. **Wrong:** I asked to him a question.
Correct: I asked him a question.
Reason: Do not use **to** after **ask** with object.

365. **Wrong:** He was died in the accident.
Correct: He died in the accident.
Reason: Die is intransitive and not used in passive.

366. **Wrong:** He speaks English fluently well.
Correct: He speaks English fluently.
Reason: Avoid redundant adverbs.

367. **Wrong:** She is working as a teacher in this school since 2019.
Correct: She has been working as a teacher in this school since 2019.
Reason: Use **present perfect continuous** with **since.**

368. **Wrong:** She is more happier now.
Correct: She is happier now.
Reason: Do not use **more** with comparatives.

369. **Wrong:** They enjoyed very much.
Correct: They enjoyed themselves very much.

Reason: Use reflexive pronoun after **enjoy** if no object.

370. **Wrong:** He is married with a doctor.
Correct: He is married to a doctor.
Reason: Use **to** with **married**.

371. **Wrong:** I am hear a sound.
Correct: I hear a sound.
Reason: **Hear** is stative and not used in continuous.

372. **Wrong:** She is more taller than me.
Correct: She is taller than me.
Reason: Avoid **more** with comparatives.

373. **Wrong:** The informations are useful.
Correct: The information is useful.
Reason: **Information** is uncountable.

374. **Wrong:** We went to picnic yesterday.
Correct: We went on a picnic yesterday.
Reason: Use **on a picnic**.

375. **Wrong:** He didn't gave the book.
Correct: He didn't give the book.
Reason: Use base verb after **didn't**.

376. **Wrong:** My friend, he is very kind.
Correct: My friend is very kind.
Reason: Avoid repeating subject.

377. **Wrong:** He is a MBA graduate.
Correct: He is an MBA graduate.
Reason: Use **an** before vowel sound.

378. **Wrong:** This is one of the best book.
Correct: This is one of the best books.
Reason: Use plural noun after **one of the**.

379. **Wrong:** He did a mistake.
Correct: He made a mistake.
Reason: Use **make a mistake**.

380. **Wrong:** I know him good.
Correct: I know him well.
Reason: Use **well** to describe manner.

381. **Wrong:** He is less taller than me.
Correct: He is shorter than me.
Reason: Use correct comparative structure.

382. **Wrong:** She is best in class.
Correct: She is the best in class.
Reason: Use **the** with superlative.

383. **Wrong:** He was angry on her.
Correct: He was angry with her.
Reason: Use **angry with**.

384. **Wrong:** The team are winning.
Correct: The team is winning.
Reason: Use singular verb with collective noun.

385. **Wrong:** He was late due to he missed the bus.
Correct: He was late because he missed the bus.
Reason: Use **because**, not **due to** + clause.

386. **Wrong:** He returned back to his village.
Correct: He returned to his village.
Reason: Avoid redundant **back**.

387. **Wrong:** She is more elder than him.
Correct: She is older than him.
Reason: Use **older**, not **more elder**.

388. **Wrong:** It is more preferable.
Correct: It is preferable.
Reason: Avoid **more preferable**.

389. **Wrong:** I am going to home.
Correct: I am going home.
Reason: Do not use **to** before **home**.

390. **Wrong:** He was very tired that he slept early.
Correct: He was so tired that he slept early.
Reason: Use **so...that** for result.

391. **Wrong:** I didn't saw him.
Correct: I didn't see him.
Reason: Use base verb after **didn't**.

392. **Wrong:** She was graduated last year.
Correct: She graduated last year.
Reason: Graduate is not used in passive voice.

393. **Wrong:** I didn't knew about it.
Correct: I didn't know about it.
Reason: Use the base verb after **didn't**.

394. **Wrong:** He is more richer than his brother.
Correct: He is richer than his brother.

Reason: Do not use **more** with comparatives.

395. **Wrong:** She suggested me to take rest.
Correct: She suggested that I take rest.
Reason: Use a clause after **suggest**.

396. **Wrong:** They are going to abroad next week.
Correct: They are going abroad next week.
Reason: **Abroad** does not take **to**.

397. **Wrong:** He didn't went there.
Correct: He didn't go there.
Reason: Use the base verb after **didn't**.

398. **Wrong:** The baby cried due to it was hungry.
Correct: The baby cried because it was hungry.
Reason: Use **because** before a clause.

399. **Wrong:** She is having two brothers.
Correct: She has two brothers.
Reason: Use **have** in the present simple for possession.

400. **Wrong:** He said me a story.
Correct: He told me a story.
Reason: **Say** does not take an indirect object.

401. **Wrong:** We discussed about politics.
Correct: We discussed politics.
Reason: Do not use **about** with **discuss**.

402. **Wrong:** I have seen her yesterday.
Correct: I saw her yesterday.
Reason: Use simple past with specific time.

403. **Wrong:** He is suffering with fever.
Correct: He has a fever.
Reason: Use **have** for medical conditions.

404. **Wrong:** I request you to kindly submit the form.
Correct: I kindly request you to submit the form.
Reason: Avoid redundant politeness.

405. **Wrong:** She has gone to the market yesterday.
Correct: She went to the market yesterday.
Reason: Use simple past with time expression.

406. **Wrong:** I do not know nothing about it.
Correct: I do not know anything about it.
Reason: Avoid double negatives.

407. **Wrong:** She is knowing the answer.
Correct: She knows the answer.
Reason: Use stative verbs in present simple.

408. **Wrong:** The teacher gave me an advice.
Correct: The teacher gave me some advice.
Reason: Advice is uncountable.

409. **Wrong:** I was born on 1997.
Correct: I was born in 1997.
Reason: Use **in** with years.

410. **Wrong:** He is in home.
Correct: He is at home.
Reason: Use **at home**.

411. **Wrong:** She is senior than me.
Correct: She is senior to me.
Reason: Use **to** with **senior**.

412. **Wrong:** He told to me the truth.
Correct: He told me the truth.
Reason: Do not use **to** after **told**.

413. **Wrong:** The furniture are old.
Correct: The furniture is old.
Reason: Furniture is uncountable.

414. **Wrong:** I look forward to meet you.
Correct: I look forward to meeting you.
Reason: Look forward to takes a gerund.

415. **Wrong:** This is a worth reading book.
Correct: This is a book worth reading.
Reason: Use the correct word order.

416. **Wrong:** She did a mistake in the report.
Correct: She made a mistake in the report.
Reason: Use **make a mistake**.

417. **Wrong:** He is lacking in confidence.
Correct: He lacks confidence.
Reason: Lack is a transitive verb.

418. **Wrong:** He asked me that why I was late.
Correct: He asked me why I was late.
Reason: Do not use **that** in indirect WH-questions.

419. **Wrong:** She denied to attend the meeting.
Correct: She denied attending the meeting.

Reason: Deny takes a gerund.

420. **Wrong:** The clock is in the wall.
Correct: The clock is on the wall.
Reason: Use the correct preposition **on**.

421. **Wrong:** He is better than all.
Correct: He is better than all others.
Reason: Use **than all others** to exclude the subject.

422. **Wrong:** She is my cousin sister.
Correct: She is my cousin.
Reason: Cousin is sufficient.

423. **Wrong:** The police is coming.
Correct: The police are coming.
Reason: Police is a plural noun.

424. **Wrong:** He is one of the best player.
Correct: He is one of the best players.
Reason: Use plural noun after **one of the**.

425. **Wrong:** He has many works to do.
Correct: He has much work to do.
Reason: Work is uncountable.

426. **Wrong:** The scenery of the hills are beautiful.
Correct: The scenery of the hills is beautiful.
Reason: Scenery is uncountable.

427. **Wrong:** I met him before two days.
Correct: I met him two days ago.
Reason: Use **ago** with time references.

428. **Wrong:** She is best in her group.
Correct: She is the best in her group.
Reason: Use **the** with superlatives.

429. **Wrong:** This is more better than that.
Correct: This is better than that.
Reason: Avoid double comparatives.

430. **Wrong:** He replied me immediately.
Correct: He replied to me immediately.
Reason: Use **to** after **reply**.

431. **Wrong:** She explained me the reason.
Correct: She explained the reason to me.
Reason: Use **to** when the indirect object follows.

432. **Wrong:** I am agree with your opinion.
Correct: I agree with your opinion.
Reason: Agree is not used with **am.**

433. **Wrong:** She can to swim well.
Correct: She can swim well.
Reason: Do not use **to** after modal verbs.

434. **Wrong:** He was died in 2005.
Correct: He died in 2005.
Reason: Die is not used in passive voice.

435. **Wrong:** He said me to wait there.
Correct: He told me to wait there.
Reason: Use **tell** for indirect commands.

436. **Wrong:** He passed out from college.
Correct: He graduated from college.
Reason: Passed out means **fainted.**

437. **Wrong:** I have a good news.
Correct: I have some good news.
Reason: News is uncountable.

438. **Wrong:** I am hearing a strange sound.
Correct: I hear a strange sound.
Reason: Hear is a stative verb.

439. **Wrong:** She told that she will come.
Correct: She said that she would come.
Reason: Use **would** in reported speech.

440. **Wrong:** He is not understanding the topic.
Correct: He doesn't understand the topic.
Reason: Use present simple for stative verbs.

441. **Wrong:** The dress is more prettier than the others.
Correct: The dress is prettier than the others.
Reason: Avoid using **more** with comparatives.

442. **Wrong:** He is my cousin brother.
Correct: He is my cousin.
Reason: Cousin already implies the relationship.

443. **Wrong:** I didn't saw him yesterday.
Correct: I didn't see him yesterday.
Reason: Use the base verb after **didn't.**

444. **Wrong:** He is my most closest friend.
Correct: He is my closest friend.

Reason: Avoid double superlatives.

445. **Wrong:** She is more friendlier than before.
Correct: She is friendlier than before.
Reason: Do not use **more** with comparatives.

446. **Wrong:** The news are shocking.
Correct: The news is shocking.
Reason: **News** is uncountable.

447. **Wrong:** He is married with a teacher.
Correct: He is married to a teacher.
Reason: Use **to** with **married**.

448. **Wrong:** I went for shopping.
Correct: I went shopping.
Reason: Do not use **for** with **shopping**.

449. **Wrong:** She is hearing a strange sound.
Correct: She hears a strange sound.
Reason: **Hear** is a stative verb.

450. **Wrong:** The information are useful.
Correct: The information is useful.
Reason: **Information** is uncountable.

451. **Wrong:** He is living here since 2010.
Correct: He has been living here since 2010.
Reason: Use **present perfect continuous** with **since**.

452. **Wrong:** She is good in dancing.
Correct: She is good at dancing.
Reason: Use **at** with **good**.

453. **Wrong:** The child is afraid from dogs.
Correct: The child is afraid of dogs.
Reason: Use **'of'** with **'afraid'**.

454. **Wrong:** I have seen her last week.
Correct: I saw her last week.
Reason: Use **simple past** with specific time.

455. **Wrong:** He didn't ate his lunch.
Correct: He didn't eat his lunch.
Reason: Use **base form** after **'didn't'**.

456. **Wrong:** He is working hardly today.
Correct: He is working hard today.
Reason: **'Hardly'** means **'barely'**.

457. **Wrong:** I didn't told you.
  Correct: I didn't tell you.
  Reason: Use **base form** after **'didn't'**.
458. **Wrong:** She resembles with her sister.
  Correct: She resembles her sister.
  Reason: Do not use **'with'** after **'resembles'**.
459. **Wrong:** She is more smarter than him.
  Correct: She is smarter than him.
  Reason: Avoid **'more'** with comparatives.
460. **Wrong:** She gave me an information.
  Correct: She gave me some information.
  Reason: **'Information'** is uncountable.
461. **Wrong:** He explained me the concept.
  Correct: He explained the concept to me.
  Reason: Use **'to'** when object follows the thing explained.
462. **Wrong:** The furniture are expensive.
  Correct: The furniture is expensive.
  Reason: **'Furniture'** is uncountable.
463. **Wrong:** He is one of the intelligent student.
  Correct: He is one of the intelligent students.
  Reason: Use **plural noun** after **'one of the'**.
464. **Wrong:** The sceneries are attractive.
  Correct: The scenery is attractive.
  Reason: **'Scenery'** is uncountable.
465. **Wrong:** I suggested him to try again.
  Correct: I suggested that he try again.
  Reason: **'Suggest'** takes a clause.
466. **Wrong:** She denied to come.
  Correct: She denied coming.
  Reason: **'Deny'** takes a gerund.
467. **Wrong:** He is graduated from university.
  Correct: He graduated from university.
  Reason: **'Graduate'** is not used in passive.
468. **Wrong:** I enjoyed at the wedding.
  Correct: I enjoyed the wedding.
  Reason: **'Enjoy'** is transitive.
469. **Wrong:** She is so beautiful girl.
  Correct: She is such a beautiful girl.

Reason: Use **'such'** with noun phrases.

470. **Wrong:** She can able to solve it.
Correct: She can solve it.
Reason: Do not use **'can'** and **'able to'** together.

471. **Wrong:** He is more stronger than me.
Correct: He is stronger than me.
Reason: Avoid **'more'** with comparatives.

472. **Wrong:** They entered into the hall.
Correct: They entered the hall.
Reason: Do not use **'into'** with **'entered'**.

473. **Wrong:** He is junior than me.
Correct: He is junior to me.
Reason: Use **'to'** with **'junior'**.

474. **Wrong:** The weather today are nice.
Correct: The weather today is nice.
Reason: **'Weather'** is uncountable.

475. **Wrong:** She was born at 1995.
Correct: She was born in 1995.
Reason: Use **'in'** with years.

476. **Wrong:** The team are winning the match.
Correct: The team is winning the match.
Reason: Use **singular verb** with collective noun.

477. **Wrong:** I didn't knew about it.
Correct: I didn't know about it.
Reason: Use **base verb** after **'didn't'**.

478. **Wrong:** She is more kinder than her sister.
Correct: She is kinder than her sister.
Reason: Avoid **'more'** with comparatives.

479. **Wrong:** He is working since morning.
Correct: He has been working since morning.
Reason: Use **present perfect continuous**.

480. **Wrong:** I have met him yesterday.
Correct: I met him yesterday.
Reason: Use **simple past** with time expressions.

481. **Wrong:** He is going to office by walk.
Correct: He is going to office on foot.
Reason: Use **'on foot'**.

482. **Wrong:** He is better than all.
     Correct: He is better than all others.
     Reason: Use **'than all others'**.
483. **Wrong:** I doubt that he will come.
     Correct: I wonder if he will come.
     Reason: Use **'wonder'** in such contexts.
484. **Wrong:** The teacher gave me many advices.
     Correct: The teacher gave me much advice.
     Reason: **'Advice'** is uncountable.
485. **Wrong:** I look forward to meet you soon.
     Correct: I look forward to meeting you soon.
     Reason: **'Look forward to'** takes a gerund.
486. **Wrong:** He did not came to class.
     Correct: He did not come to class.
     Reason: Use **base verb** after **'did not'**.
487. **Wrong:** She was graduated last year.
     Correct: She graduated last year.
     Reason: **'Graduate'** is not used in passive.
488. **Wrong:** She is listening music.
     Correct: She is listening to music.
     Reason: Use **'to'** with **'listen'**.
489. **Wrong:** The building comprises of five floors.
     Correct: The building comprises five floors.
     Reason: Do not use **'of'** after **'comprises'**.
490. **Wrong:** I have no any doubt.
     Correct: I have no doubt.
     Reason: Do not use **'no'** and **'any'** together.
491. **Wrong:** He didn't wanted to go.
     Correct: He didn't want to go.
     Reason: Use **base form** after **'didn't'**.

CHAPTER THREE

SAMPLE LETTERS

Sample Letters for Teachers for Various Situations

1. Leave Letter (Sick Leave)

Date: [Insert Date]
Chennai
From:
    R. Rani Sasikala
    Assistant Teacher
    XYZ Government School
    Chennai – 600001
To:
    The Headmaster
    XYZ Government School
    Chennai – 600001

Subject: Request for Sick Leave

Respected Sir/Madam,

    I am writing to inform you that I am suffering from a high fever and have been advised bed rest by my doctor. I kindly request that you grant me sick leave for three days from 20 May to 22 May 2025.

Thank you for being so understanding.

Yours sincerely,
R. Rani Sasikala

2. *Casual Leave Letter*

Date: [Insert Date]
Chennai
From:
  R. Rani Sasikala
  Assistant Teacher
  XYZ Government School
  Chennai – 600001
To:
   The Headmaster
   XYZ Government School
   Chennai – 600001

Subject: Request for Casual Leave

Respected Sir/Madam,
                I wish to take a casual leave on 24th May 2026 due to a personal commitment. Kindly grant me leave for one day.
Thank you for your consideration.

Yours faithfully,
 R. Rani Sasikala

3. *Permission to Attend Workshop*

Date: [Insert Date]
Chennai
From:
  R. Rani Sasikala
  Assistant Teacher
  XYZ Government School
  Chennai – 600001

To:
The Headmaster
XYZ Government School
Chennai – 600001

Subject: Request for Permission to Attend Educational Workshop

Respected Sir/Madam,

I am pleased to inform you that I have been invited to attend a teacher training workshop on "Innovative Teaching Techniques" organized by the District Education Office on 27th May 2026. I kindly request permission to attend this workshop as it would enhance my professional skills.

I assure you that I will make up for any missed responsibilities during my absence.

Thanking you.

Yours sincerely,
R. Rani Sasikala

4. Appreciation Letter to Students

Date: [Insert Date]
Chennai
From:
R. Rani Sasikala
Class Teacher
XYZ Government School
Chennai – 600001
To:
Class VIII Students
XYZ Government School
Chennai – 600001

Subject: Congratulations on Excellent Performance

Dear Students,

I am extremely proud of your outstanding performance in the recent examinations. Your hard work and determination have brought great pride to our class.

Keep up the excellent work!

Warm regards,
R. Rani Sasikala

5. Complaint Letter to HM (e.g., Infrastructure Issue)

Date: [Insert Date]
Chennai
From:
R. Rani Sasikala
Assistant Teacher
XYZ Government School
Chennai – 600001
To:
The Headmaster
XYZ Government School
Chennai – 600001

Subject: Complaint Regarding Damaged Classroom Ceiling

Respected Sir/Madam,

I would like to bring to your attention the deteriorating condition of the ceiling in Class VI-B. The roof has developed cracks, and during rains, water seeps in, causing inconvenience and safety concerns for students.

Kindly take the necessary steps to have the issue resolved at the earliest. Thanking you.

Yours faithfully,
R. Rani Sasikala

6. *Request Letter for Stationery*

Date: [Insert Date]
Chennai
From:
   R. Rani Sasikala
   Assistant Teacher
   XYZ Government School
   Chennai – 600001
To:
   The Headmaster
   XYZ Government School
   Chennai – 600001

Subject: Request for Teaching Stationery

Respected Sir/Madam,
            I kindly request you to provide basic teaching materials such as whiteboard markers, chart papers, and A4 sheets for classroom activities. These materials are essential to carry out interactive learning sessions.
Thanking you in anticipation.

Yours sincerely,
 R. Rani Sasikala

7. *Letter to Parents (Progress Update)*

Date: [Insert Date]
Chennai
From:
   R. Rani Sasikala
   Class Teacher
   XYZ Government School
   Chennai – 600001
To:
   Parents of Class VI-A Students

XYZ Government School
Chennai – 600001

Subject: Student Progress Update

Dear Parent,

This is to inform you that your child is progressing steadily in academics and co-curricular activities. However, regular attendance and daily revision are essential for continued success.

Please feel free to contact me during school hours for any clarification.

Sincerely,
R. Rani Sasikala

8. *Letter of Introduction (to Parents)*

Date: [Insert Date]
Chennai
From:
R. Rani Sasikala
Class Teacher – V-A
XYZ Government School
Chennai – 600001
To:
Parents of Class V-A
XYZ Government School
Chennai – 600001

Subject: Self-Introduction

Dear Parent,

I am R. Rani Sasikala, the new class teacher for your child's section (Class V-A). I look forward to working closely with you to support your child's education and overall development.

Please feel free to communicate with me on any concerns or suggestions.

Warm regards,
R. Rani Sasikala

9. Application for Transfer (Internal)

Date: [Insert Date]
Chennai
From:
R. Rani Sasikala
Assistant Teacher
XYZ Government School
Chennai – 600001
To:
The Headmaster
XYZ Government School
Chennai – 600001

Subject: Application for Internal Transfer

Respected Sir/Madam,

I hereby request a transfer to the English Department due to my educational background and interest in literature. I am confident that I can contribute effectively in that role.

I would be grateful if my request is considered favorably.
Thanking you.

Yours faithfully,
R. Rani Sasikala

10. Retirement Letter (Advance Notice)

Date: [Insert Date]
Chennai
From:
R. Rani Sasikala
Assistant Teacher

XYZ Government School
Chennai – 600001
To:
The Headmaster
XYZ Government School
Chennai – 600001

Subject: Notice of Retirement

Respected Sir/Madam,

I wish to formally inform you of my intent to retire from service on 30th June 2026. I have enjoyed my tenure and am thankful for the support and opportunities extended to me.

Please let me know the necessary procedures to complete the formalities.

With sincere gratitude,
R. Rani Sasikala

11. Resignation Letter

Date: [Insert Date]
Chennai
From:
R. Rani Sasikala
Assistant Teacher
ABC Matriculation School
Chennai – 600 001
To:
The Principal
ABC Matriculation School
Chennai – 600 001

Subject: Resignation Letter

Dear Sir/Madam,

I am writing to formally resign from my position as Assistant Teacher at ABC Matriculation School, effective [Last Working Day, e.g., 30th June 2025].

It has been a great pleasure and privilege to be part of the school community. I am thankful for the support and opportunities I have received during my tenure, and I truly appreciate the guidance and encouragement from the management and staff.

This decision has not been easy, but it is taken after careful consideration of my personal and professional goals.

Please consider this letter as my official notice, and I am happy to assist in the transition period in any way possible.

Thank you once again for the valuable experiences.

Yours sincerely,
  R. Rani Sasikala

II. Sample Leave Letters for Various Situations

1. Leave for Personal Work

Date: [Insert Date]
Chennai
From:
   R. Rani Sasikala
   Assistant Teacher
   XYZ Government School
   Chennai – 600001
To:
   The Headmaster
   XYZ Government School
   Chennai – 600001

Subject: Request for Leave for Personal Work

Respected Sir/Madam,

I kindly request leave for one day on [insert date] due to an urgent personal matter that requires my attention. Kindly grant me leave for the mentioned date.

I appreciate your understanding.

Yours faithfully,
R. Rani Sasikala

2. *Leave for Family Function*

Date: [Insert Date]
Chennai
From:
  R. Rani Sasikala
  Assistant Teacher
  XYZ Government School
  Chennai – 600001
To:
  The Headmaster
  XYZ Government School
  Chennai – 600001

Subject: Request for Leave to Attend a Family Function

Respected Sir/Madam,

I wish to inform you that I have to attend a family function on [insert date]. I request you to kindly grant me leave for one day so I can attend the event.

Thank you in advance.

Yours sincerely,
R. Rani Sasikala

3. *Leave for Child's Illness*

Date: [Insert Date]

Chennai
From:
  R. Rani Sasikala
  Assistant Teacher
  XYZ Government School
  Chennai – 600001
To:
  The Headmaster
  XYZ Government School
  Chennai – 600001

Subject: Request for Leave Due to My Child's Illness

Respected Sir/Madam,

           I am writing to inform you that my child is unwell and requires my care and attention. Hence, I request leave for [insert date or duration].

Thank you for your kind consideration.

Yours faithfully,
  R. Rani Sasikala

4. *Maternity Leave Application*

Date: [Insert Date]
Chennai
From:
  R. Rani Sasikala
  Assistant Teacher
  XYZ Government School
  Chennai – 600001
To:
  The Headmaster
  XYZ Government School
  Chennai – 600001

Subject: Application for Maternity Leave

Respected Sir/Madam,

I am writing to formally request maternity leave starting from [insert start date] as per the medical advice. I kindly request you to grant me leave for the recommended period.

Thank you for your support and consideration.

Yours sincerely,

R. Rani Sasikala

5. Leave for Exam Duty

Date: [Insert Date]

Chennai

From:

R. Rani Sasikala

Assistant Teacher

XYZ Government School

Chennai – 600001

To:

The Headmaster

XYZ Government School

Chennai – 600001

Subject: Request for Leave for External Exam Duty

Respected Sir/Madam,

I have been assigned invigilation duties at [insert institution name] on [insert date]. I kindly request you to consider this as duty leave and grant permission to be absent on that day.

Yours faithfully,

R. Rani Sasikala

6. Leave for Attending a Marriage

Date: [Insert Date]

Chennai

From:
R. Rani Sasikala
Assistant Teacher
XYZ Government School
Chennai – 600001
To:
The Headmaster
XYZ Government School
Chennai – 600001

Subject: Leave Request to Attend a Wedding Ceremony
Respected Sir/Madam,

I humbly request leave on [insert date] as I will be attending a close relative's marriage. Kindly grant me leave for the stated purpose.

Thanking you.
Yours sincerely,
R. Rani Sasikala

7. Emergency Leave

Date: [Insert Date]
Chennai
From:
R. Rani Sasikala
Assistant Teacher
XYZ Government School
Chennai – 600001
To:
The Headmaster
XYZ Government School
Chennai – 600001

Subject: Application for Emergency Leave
Respected Sir/Madam,

Due to an unforeseen emergency at home, I am unable to attend school on [insert date]. I request you to kindly grant me emergency leave.

   Thanking you for your support.

   Yours faithfully,

     R. Rani Sasikala

8. *Leave for Religious Observance*

Date: [Insert Date]

Chennai

From:

   R. Rani Sasikala

   Assistant Teacher

   XYZ Government School

   Chennai – 600001

To:

   The Headmaster

   XYZ Government School

   Chennai – 600001

Subject: Request for Leave for Religious Observance

Respected Sir/Madam,

           I wish to request leave on [insert date] to participate in a religious ceremony. Kindly grant me leave for the mentioned day.

   I appreciate your understanding.

   Yours sincerely,

     R. Rani Sasikala

III. *Asking Leave for Various Family Functions*

1. *Leave a Letter for Attending a Wedding*

Date: [Insert Date]

Chennai

From:

   R. Indumathi

Assistant Teacher
XYZ Government School
Chennai – 600001
To:
The Headmaster
XYZ Government School
Chennai – 600001

Subject: Leave Request for Attending a Family Wedding

Respected Sir/Madam,

I am writing to request leave from [Start Date] to [End Date] as I need to attend the wedding of a close family member in [Location]. My presence is essential for the occasion.
I kindly request you to grant me [number of days] days of leave. I will ensure that my responsibilities are managed during my absence.
Thank you for your consideration.

Yours sincerely,
R. Indumathi

2. *Leave Letter for Housewarming Ceremony*

Date: [Insert Date]
Chennai
From:
R. Indumathi
Assistant Teacher
XYZ Government School
Chennai – 600001
To:
The Headmaster
XYZ Government School
Chennai – 600001

Subject: Request for Leave for Housewarming Ceremony

Respected Sir/Madam,

I respectfully request leave on [Date] as we are conducting the housewarming ceremony of our new residence. My presence is required for the event and related preparations.

Please grant me leave for [number of days] days. I will resume duties on [Return Date].

Thanking you.

Yours sincerely,
R. Indumathi

3. Leave Letter for Naming Ceremony

Date: [Insert Date]
Chennai
From:
R. Indumathi
Assistant Teacher
XYZ Government School
Chennai – 600001
To:
The Headmaster
XYZ Government School
Chennai – 600001

Subject: Leave Request for Attending Naming Ceremony

Respected Sir/Madam,

I would like to request leave on [Date] to attend the naming ceremony of my [relation, e.g., niece/nephew]. It is a significant family function, and I am expected to take part.

Kindly grant me leave for [number of days] days.

Thank you for your kind approval.

Yours sincerely,
R. Indumathi

4. Leave Letter for Engagement Function

Date: [Insert Date]
Chennai
From:
  R. Indumathi
  Assistant Teacher
  XYZ Government School
  Chennai – 600001
To:
   The Headmaster
  XYZ Government School
  Chennai – 600001

Subject: Leave Application for Attending Engagement Function

Dear Sir/Madam,
          I would like to request leave from [Start Date] to [End Date] to attend the engagement ceremony of my [relation – e.g., sister/cousin]. Kindly consider my request and grant me leave for [number of days] days. I will resume my work on [Return Date].

Yours sincerely,
 R. Indumathi

5. Leave Letter for Attending a Pooja (Religious Ceremony)

Date: [Insert Date]
Chennai
From:
  R. Indumathi
  Assistant Teacher
  XYZ Government School
  Chennai – 600001

To:

The Headmaster
XYZ Government School
Chennai – 600001

Subject: Leave Request for Attending Family Pooja

Respected Sir/Madam,

I would like to request leave on [Date] to attend a religious pooja being held at our home. It is a traditional family event, and I am required to participate.
Kindly grant me leave for the day.
Thank you for your kind consideration.

Yours sincerely,
R. Indumathi

CHAPTER FOUR

REMARKS FOR RANK CARDS

1. Excellent performance. Keep it up!
2. Very good progress throughout the term.
3. Shows consistent effort and interest.
4. A hardworking and sincere student.
5. Performs well in all subjects.
6. Needs to participate more actively in class.
7. Good understanding of concepts.
8. Has shown commendable improvement.
9. Keep working hard to maintain your rank.
10. A disciplined and well-mannered student.
11. Demonstrates leadership qualities.
12. Good in both academics and co-curricular activities.
13. Needs to focus more on Mathematics.
14. Excellent in communication skills.
15. A creative and enthusiastic learner.
16. Needs to improve handwriting.
17. Should revise lessons regularly.
18. Must submit assignments on time.
19. Keep up the positive attitude.
20. Shows great potential.
21. Must concentrate more during lessons.
22. A polite and cooperative student.
23. Very attentive and eager to learn.

24. Good improvement in reading skills.
25. Should participate more in group activities.
26. Needs to improve in Science.
27. Has a positive attitude toward learning.
28. A well-behaved student.
29. A role model for classmates.
30. Continue the excellent academic journey!
31. Excellent performance. Keep it up!
32. Very good progress throughout the term.
33. Shows consistent effort and interest.
34. A hardworking and sincere student.
35. Performs well in all subjects.
36. Needs to participate more actively in class.
37. Good understanding of concepts.
38. Has shown commendable improvement.
39. Keep working hard to maintain your rank.
40. A disciplined and well-mannered student.
41. Demonstrates leadership qualities.
42. Good in both academics and co-curricular activities.
43. Needs to focus more on Mathematics.
44. Excellent in communication skills.
45. A creative and enthusiastic learner.
46. Needs to improve handwriting.
47. Should revise lessons regularly.
48. Must submit assignments on time.
49. Keep up the positive attitude.
50. Shows great potential.
51. Must concentrate more during lessons.
52. A polite and cooperative student.
53. Very attentive and eager to learn.
54. Good improvement in reading skills.
55. Should participate more in group activities.
56. Needs to improve in Science.
57. Has a positive attitude toward learning.
58. A well-behaved student.
59. A role model for classmates.
60. Continue the excellent academic journey!
61. Completes assignments with care.

62. Brings energy and enthusiasm to the class.
63. A quiet yet dedicated learner.
64. Demonstrates responsibility in group work.
65. Needs to participate more in discussions.
66. Excellent behaviour and attitude.
67. Capable student who needs to believe in self.
68. A creative thinker and problem solver.
69. Keeps class materials well-organized.
70. Should aim for higher academic targets.
71. Has improved significantly this term.
72. Needs to revise lessons more frequently.
73. Should avoid careless spelling errors.
74. Demonstrates empathy and kindness.
75. Strong memory and recall ability.
76. Can be a great leader with guidance.
77. Needs to manage time better during exams.
78. Brings a positive spirit to class.
79. Follows instructions well.
80. Shows improvement in oral presentations.
81. Encouraged to take part in competitions.
82. Should work on vocabulary development.
83. Listens well and follows directions.
84. Needs to show more initiative.
85. Shows interest in science experiments.
86. Good handwriting and presentation skills.
87. Enjoys classroom challenges.
88. Tends to rush through tasks—should slow down.
89. Can achieve more with better focus.
90. Has a cheerful and helpful nature.
91. Applies feedback to improve work.
92. A dependable class member.
93. Strong in mathematics and logical thinking.
94. Needs to stay motivated.
95. Reads fluently with expression.
96. A keen observer in class activities.
97. Keeps improving in grammar and usage.
98. Enjoys creative writing tasks.
99. Often supports classmates with kindness.

100. Ready for the next level of learning.

101. Always tries to do her best in every subject.

102. Makes steady progress with consistent effort.

103. Works independently with minimal supervision.

104. Participates actively in class discussions.

105. Needs to work on organizing thoughts clearly in writing.

106. Shows creativity in problem-solving tasks.

107. A confident learner who asks thoughtful questions.

108. Demonstrates good digital literacy skills.

109. Responds positively to feedback and guidance.

110. Has developed good study habits this term.

111. Needs to read instructions more carefully.

112. Expresses ideas clearly and effectively.

113. Shows an excellent attitude toward learning.

114. An eager participant in group projects.

115. Handles responsibilities with maturity.

116. Needs to improve time management during classwork.

117. Regular practice will help improve academic performance.

118. Demonstrates a growth mindset.

119. Is respectful to peers and teachers alike.

120. Always ready to lend a helping hand.

121. Enjoys exploring new ideas and concepts.

122. Is developing leadership skills through teamwork.

123. Enthusiastic about classroom learning.

124. Could benefit from reading more regularly.

125. Positive approach enhances class environment.

126. Needs to put more effort into revision.

127. Can excel further with consistent practice.

128. Demonstrates resilience when faced with challenges.

129. Capable of producing excellent work with focus.

130. Has grown more confident this term.

131. Shows initiative in independent learning.

132. An inquisitive mind with great potential.

133. Continues to strengthen foundational skills.

134. Shows maturity in decision-making.

135. Displays excellent group collaboration skills.

136. Works diligently to meet academic goals.

137. Makes thoughtful contributions during discussions.

138. More attention to detail will boost accuracy.

139. Demonstrates good emotional intelligence.

140. Applies classroom learning in real-life situations.

141. Developing stronger research and inquiry skills.

142. Completes tasks on time and with care.

143. A well-rounded and thoughtful student.

144. Should aim to avoid distractions during lessons.

145. Becoming more confident in speaking up.

146. Values classroom rules and expectations.

147. Improving at expressing thoughts in writing.

148. Active listener who responds appropriately.

149. Shows increasing enthusiasm for learning.

150. Demonstrates steady academic growth.

151. Accepts challenges and takes them as learning opportunities.

152. Beginning to show more confidence in classwork.

153. Should maintain consistency in homework completion.

154. Demonstrates growing independence in learning.

155. Encouraged to revise regularly for better retention.

156. Stays calm and focused under pressure.

157. Is steadily improving across all subjects.

158. A quiet achiever with strong potential.

159. Completes all tasks with sincerity and dedication.

160. Regular revision has shown good results.

161. Is capable of achieving more with greater effort.

162. Pays close attention during instruction.

163. Has started participating more in classroom tasks.

164. Always eager to try new learning activities.

165. Shows self-motivation in completing tasks.

166. Often shares insightful thoughts during lessons.

167. Should focus more on presentation skills.

168. A respectful and attentive listener.

169. Can improve further with better time allocation.

170. Frequently asks meaningful and relevant questions.

171. Strives to improve and welcomes feedback.

172. Shows a balanced approach to academics and hobbies.

173. Needs to be more consistent in class attendance.

174. Often shows originality in project work.

175. A joyful presence in the classroom.

176. Responds well to constructive criticism.

177. Makes commendable efforts in collaborative activities.

178. Demonstrates a positive attitude toward challenges.

179. Regular practice is beginning to show in results.

180. Shows increasing responsibility in academics.

181. Builds good relationships with classmates.

182. Needs to pay more attention to written work.

183. Seeks clarification when needed—an excellent trait.

184. Responds positively to classroom expectations.

185. Exhibits creativity in visual and written tasks.

186. Has developed good speaking and listening skills.

187. Beginning to display leadership in peer groups.

188. Should aim for neater written presentations.

189. Demonstrates awareness and respect for rules.

190. Is courteous and considerate in interactions.

191. Able to work effectively both alone and with others.

192. Often contributes fresh ideas to discussions.

193. Starting to take greater ownership of learning.

194. Could benefit from setting academic goals.

195. A motivated student with strong aspirations.

196. Consistently shows good manners and discipline.

197. Enjoys discovering new knowledge independently.

198. Displays effort even in unfamiliar tasks.

199. Can reach greater heights with focused attention.

200. Ready to explore new academic challenges ahead.

CHAPTER FIVE

COMMONLY MISSPELT WORDS

Here is a list of commonly misspelt words along with their correct spellings:

Misspelt Correct

acheive – achieve
adress – address
beggining – beginning
calender – calendar
definately – definitely
embarass – embarrass
enviroment – environment
exagerate – exaggerate
goverment – government
grammer – grammar
happend – happened
hight – height
independant – independent
inteligent – intelligent
interupt – interrupt
knowlege – knowledge
libary – library
mischievious – mischievous
neccessary – necessary
occurence – occurrence
ocasionaly – occasionally

paralel – parallel
posession – possession
preceed – precede
recieve – receive
recomend – recommend
relevent – relevant
seperate – separate
sucess – success
surprize – surprise
tommorow – tomorrow
tounge – tongue
truely – truly
untill – until
vaccum – vacuum
wierd – weird
writting – writing
accesory – accessory
acurate – accurate
arguement – argument
beleive – believe
buisness – business
carrers – careers
concious – conscious
curiousity – curiosity
descision – decision
dissapoint – disappoint
exageration – exaggeration
exersize – exercise
foriegn – foreign
freind – friend
guage – gauge
heared – heard
heirarchy – hierarchy
hounour – honour
imediate – immediate
improvment – improvement
independance – independence
intergrate – integrate

intersting – interesting
irrelevent – irrelevant
judgement – judgment
knowledege – knowledge
labled – labelled
leisure – leisure
maintanance – maintenance
mathamatics – mathematics
millenium – millennium
mispell – misspell
neice – niece
noticable – noticeable
occasian – occasion
occuring – occurring
offical – official
overide – override
partener – partner
persue – pursue
posative – positive
preperation – preparation
pronounciation – pronunciation
proffessor – professor
publically – publicly
quesionnaire – questionnaire
recieveing – receiving
rediculous – ridiculous
refered – referred
relevence – relevance
religous – religious
repitition – repetition
resistence – resistance
rythm – rhythm
scedule – schedule
secratary – secretary
sentance – sentence
seperate – separate
similiar – similar
speach – speech

sponsership – sponsorship
strenth – strength
sucessful – successful
surprized – surprised
tatoo – tattoo
tution – tuition
twelth – twelfth
unfortunatly – unfortunately
untill – until
vaccuum – vacuum
visious – vicious
wierdly – weirdly
writen – written
acheived – achieved
ammount – amount
apparant – apparent
arguementative – argumentative
atempt – attempt
bizzare – bizarre
calendered – calendared
cemetary – cemetery
charactor – character
clumsyest – clumsiest
colect – collect
comparision – comparison
conceed – concede
congradulations – congratulations
convienient – convenient
correspondant – correspondent
curiculum – curriculum
dessicate – desiccate
disapear – disappear
dissapearence – disappearance
eficient – efficient
embarased – embarrassed
equiptment – equipment
exagerating – exaggerating
familier – familiar

fascinateing – fascinating
finaly – finally
floride – fluoride
forcast – forecast
fortunatly – fortunately
freindship – friendship
fustrate – frustrate
garentee – guarantee
geneticaly – genetically
governer – governor
guidlines – guidelines
happyness – happiness
higer – higher
hygeine – hygiene
identicle – identical
ignorence – ignorance
immediatly – immediately
incidently – incidentally
inteligence – intelligence
interveiwer – interviewer
invatation – invitation
jealouse – jealous
knowhow – know-how
lier – liar
literaly – literally
maintaine – maintain
manualy – manually
mathmatical – mathematical
measurment – measurement
mischievious – mischievous
mispellings – misspellings
neuclear – nuclear
occurance – occurrence
oppurtunity – opportunity
orignal – original
paralell – parallel
particulary – particularly
pasttime – pastime

peom – poem
permanant – permanent
plesant – pleasant
poisenous – poisonous
politition – politician
possable – possible
preist – priest
presance – presence
privilage – privilege
pronounciate – pronounce
propably – probably
quantaty – quantity
queston – question
reciept – receipt
recomendation – recommendation
refference – reference
religon – religion
remmember – remember
resque – rescue
restaurante – restaurant
ritch – rich
saftey – safety
scenerio – scenario
secretery – secretary
seperation – separation
shcool – school
signifacant – significant

CHAPTER SIX

DIALOGUE BETWEEN TEACHER AND STUDENTS

Topic: Classroom Discipline and Homework

Teacher: Good morning, class.

Students: Good morning, ma'am.

Teacher: I hope you all had a good weekend. Let's begin with a quick check—how many of you have completed your homework?

Student A: I have, ma'am.

Student B: Sorry ma'am, I forgot.

Teacher: It's important to be responsible and finish your homework on time. Can you tell me why homework is given?

Student C: To help us revise what we learnt in class.

Teacher: Exactly. Homework reinforces learning. Those who haven't completed it, please submit it by tomorrow without fail.

Student B: Yes, ma'am. I will complete it today.

Teacher: Good. Now, one more thing—please remember not to talk when someone else is speaking. It's important to respect others.

Student D: Sorry ma'am, we will be careful.

Teacher: Thank you. Now let's move on to today's lesson. Open your English textbooks to page 42.

Topic: *Exam Preparation*

Teacher: The exams are approaching. Are you all preparing regularly?
Student A: Yes, ma'am. We've made a study timetable.
Teacher: That's excellent. Revision is the key. Don't forget to solve past question papers too.
Student B: Will you be conducting a revision test, ma'am?
Teacher: Yes, next Monday. So be prepared. Start revising from today itself. I will also give you a revision worksheet.
Student C: Ma'am, could you revise the important topics in tomorrow's class?
Teacher: Certainly. Tomorrow we'll go over the grammar section and writing skills.
Student D: Should we bring any materials for revision?
Teacher: Bring your notebooks, past worksheets, and the grammar book. Also, prepare any doubts you want to clarify.
Student A: Will the exam pattern be the same as last term?
Teacher: Mostly, yes. But some sections will be a bit more analytical. I'll explain the paper pattern in detail tomorrow.
Student B: Thank you, ma'am. That helps a lot.
Teacher: You're welcome. Now let's begin today's lesson with a quick recap.

Topic: *Class Cleanliness*

Teacher: Children, I see some papers on the floor. Who will help clean the classroom?
Students: We will, ma'am!
Teacher: That's the spirit! Keeping the class clean is everyone's responsibility. Clean surroundings help us stay healthy and learn better.
Student A: I can sweep today, ma'am.
Teacher: Thank you. And who will wipe the board?
Student B: I will do it, ma'am.
Teacher: Wonderful! From now on, we will make a weekly duty chart. Every student will take turns keeping the classroom clean.
Student C: Can we also decorate the class board?

Teacher: That's a great idea! Let's plan a board decoration activity on Friday. Clean class, happy class!
Students: Yes, ma'am!**Topic: Library Period**
Teacher: Today is your library period. Please pick a book of your interest.
Student A: Ma'am, can you suggest a storybook for me?
Teacher: Sure, try "The Blue Umbrella" by Ruskin Bond. It's a lovely story.
Student B: Can we exchange books after a week?
Teacher: Yes, you can. Just make sure to return the book in good condition.

Topic: Field Trip Announcement

Teacher: We are planning a field trip next Friday. Who is excited?
Students: Yay! We are, ma'am!
Teacher: You will receive a permission slip today. Ask your parents to sign it and return it by Wednesday. Wear comfortable clothes and bring your lunch.
Student A: Ma'am, where are we going?
Teacher: We will be visiting the Science and Technology Museum. There will be guided tours and interactive exhibits.
Student B: Can we bring snacks?
Teacher: Yes, but pack only dry items and water. Avoid chips and sugary drinks.
Student C: Will we be back before school ends?
Teacher: Yes, we will leave after morning assembly and return by 3:30 p.m.
Student D: Can we carry cameras or mobile phones?
Teacher: No cameras or phones are allowed. You can enjoy and observe. We'll be taking pictures as a group.
Student A: This sounds fun!
Teacher: I'm glad you're excited! Follow the rules, and we'll all have a great time. Who is excited?
Students: Yay! We are, ma'am!
Teacher: You will receive a permission slip today. Ask your parents to sign it and return it by Wednesday. Wear comfortable clothes and bring your lunch.

Topic: Morning Assembly Preparation

Teacher: Our class is hosting the assembly this week. Who would like to volunteer for the speech?
Student B: I would, ma'am!
Teacher: Wonderful. Anyone else for prayer, thought, or news reading?
Student C: I'll do the news, ma'am.
Student D: Ma'am, I can say the thought for the day.
Teacher: Excellent! Thank you for volunteering. We'll divide the time and practice during the activity period.
Student A: Will we get a script, ma'am?
Teacher: Yes, I will give you your parts today. Make sure to practice your lines and speak clearly.
Student C: Will we have a mic for the news reading?
Teacher: Yes, you will. I'll coordinate with the staff to arrange everything. Just focus on speaking slowly and confidently.
Student B: I'm a little nervous.
Teacher: That's okay. It's natural. Just rehearse well and imagine you are talking to your friends. You'll do great!
Students: Thank you, ma'am!
Teacher: Let's make this assembly memorable. I'm proud of your enthusiasm!

Topic: Discipline Reminder

Teacher: There has been too much noise lately. Let's remember our classroom rules.
Student A: Sorry ma'am, we will stay quiet and listen.
Teacher: Thank you. A peaceful class helps everyone learn better. We must all be respectful and give everyone a chance to learn.
Student B: Sometimes we get too excited and talk loudly, ma'am.
Teacher: I understand. It's okay to be excited, but we must control our voices. When someone is speaking, others must listen.
Student C: What should we do if someone disturbs us during class?
Teacher: That's a good question. If someone disturbs you, raise your hand

and let me know. Never shout or argue in class.

Student D: Can we remind each other gently?

Teacher: Yes, but always use polite language. We should help each other become better students.

Student A: Okay ma'am, we'll follow the rules.

Teacher: Wonderful. Let's all try our best to make this classroom a calm and happy place for learning.

Topic: Birthday Celebration

Teacher: Whose birthday is today?

Student: It's mine, ma'am.

Teacher: Happy Birthday! Let's all wish and sing for your friend.

Students: Happy Birthday to you...!

Teacher: Do you want to share a few words?

Student: Thank you, ma'am. I'm happy to celebrate it with my friends.

Teacher: That's lovely. May you have a joyful and successful year ahead.

Student B: Ma'am, can we decorate the class board with a birthday card?

Teacher: That's a thoughtful idea! Let's make a quick card during the activity period.

Student C: Can we take a class photo with our friend?

Teacher: Sure, we can take one after class as a memory. Now, let's settle down and continue with our lesson.

Topic: Checking Attendance

Teacher: Let me take attendance. If you're here, please say 'Present'.

Students: Present, ma'am!

Teacher: Good to see everyone present today. Let's aim for full attendance all week.

Student A: Ma'am, what happens if someone is late?

Teacher: If you're late, you must report to the office and bring a late slip.

Try to be punctual.

Student B: What if we're absent due to illness?

Teacher: You must bring a leave letter signed by your parents when you return. It helps us keep proper records.

Student C: Can attendance affect our grades?

Teacher: Yes, regular attendance is part of your overall performance. It shows discipline and commitment.

Student D: We'll try to come every day, ma'am.

Teacher: That's the spirit! Let's continue with our lesson now.

Topic: *Prize Distribution Appreciation*

Teacher: Congratulations to all the winners of the competition!

Student A: Thank you, ma'am.

Teacher: We are all proud of you. Let's clap for our classmates. To others, keep participating and trying your best.

Student B: Ma'am, will the winners get certificates?

Teacher: Yes, certificates and prizes will be distributed during the morning assembly on Friday.

Student C: Can we see the list of winners?

Teacher: Sure. I'll put it up on the class noticeboard.

Student D: I participated but didn't win.

Teacher: That's alright. What matters most is your effort. Keep improving and participate again.

Student D: I will try harder next time, ma'am.

Teacher: That's the spirit! I believe every one of you has great potential.

Topic: *End of the Day Review*

Teacher: What did we learn today in English class?

Student B: We learnt how to write a letter.

Teacher: That's right. Who can tell me the parts of a formal letter?

Student C: Sender's address, date, recipient's address, subject, salutation, body, and closing.

Teacher: Well done! Why is each part important?

Student D: The address and date show when and where the letter was written.

Student A: The subject tells what the letter is about.

Teacher: Excellent answers! A good structure helps the reader understand the message clearly.

Student B: Ma'am, can we get a sample letter to refer to?

Teacher: Yes, I'll write one on the board tomorrow, and we'll discuss it together.

Student C: Do we have to write it in our notebooks?

Teacher: Yes, please write the sample letter neatly in your English notebook. It will help you during revision.

Teacher: Now, pack your bags and make sure your desk is tidy.

Students: Yes, ma'am!

Teacher: See you all tomorrow. Have a good evening!

CHAPTER SEVEN

WH Questions in the Classroom Context

Definition of WH-Questions:

WH-questions are questions that begin with a **question word** starting with '**wh**' (like *what, where, when, who, which, why*) or **how**. These questions ask for **information** rather than just a **yes or no** answer.

? **WH Question Words and Their Use:**

What

Asks about things

What is your name?

Where

Asks about place

Where do you live?

When

Asks about time

When is the meeting?

Who

Asks about a person (subject)

Who called you?

Whom

Asks about a person (object)

Whom did you meet?

Which

Asks to choose between options

Which book do you prefer?

Why
Asks about reason
Why are you late?
How
Asks about manner/condition
How do you cook pasta?
Structure of WH-Questions:
1. WH + Auxiliary + Subject + Main Verb

- *Where **do** you live?*
- *Why **did** she leave early?*

2. WH + Verb (when 'who' is the subject)

- *Who wrote this poem?*
- *What happened yesterday?*

WH Questions in the Classroom Context

1. Q: What is the topic for today?
   A: The topic is 'Parts of Speech'.
2. Q: Who will present the answer?
   A: Rahul will present the answer.
3. Q: When is the homework due?
   A: The homework is due tomorrow.
4. Q: Where should I write the answer?
   A: Write the answer in your English notebook.
5. Q: Why is punctuation important?
   A: It helps make sentences clear and meaningful.
6. Q: How do we start a formal letter?
   A: We start with the sender's address and date.
7. Q: What did we learn yesterday?
   A: We learned how to write informal letters.
8. Q: Who can tell me the correct spelling?
   A: I can, ma'am—it's 'separate'.
9. Q: When will we have the test?
   A: The test is on Friday.

10. Q: Where do we submit our notebooks?

    A: Submit them on the teacher's table.

11. Q: Why should we revise regularly?

    A: It helps us remember better.

12. Q: How can I improve my handwriting?

    A: Practice daily and write slowly and neatly.

13. Q: What is the correct answer?

    A: The correct answer is option B.

14. Q: Who wants to volunteer for reading?

    A: I do, ma'am!

15. Q: When does the library period start?

    A: It starts at 11:00 AM.

16. Q: Where is our field trip destination?

    A: We are going to the Science Museum.

17. Q: Why is attendance important?

    A: It shows commitment and regularity.

18. Q: How many marks is this question?

    A: It carries 5 marks.

19. Q: What should we bring tomorrow?

    A: Bring your geometry box and notebook.

20. Q: Who forgot their homework today?

    A: I forgot, ma'am. Sorry!

21. Q: What is your doubt in this topic?

    A: I don't understand the last exercise.

22. Q: Who was absent yesterday?

    A: Ramesh was absent, ma'am.

23. Q: When should we submit the project?

    A: It should be submitted by Monday.

24. Q: Where do we paste the chart?

    A: On the display board near the entrance.

25. Q: Why do we need to read aloud?

    A: It helps improve pronunciation and confidence.

26. Q: How do you solve this equation?

    A: By using the formula for area.

27. Q: What did you understand from the poem?

    A: It's about nature and peace.

28. Q: Who is the class leader?

    A: Anitha is our class leader.

29. Q: When do we get the corrected papers?
    A: You'll get them next Thursday.
30. Q: Where can I find my missing book?
    A: Check the lost-and-found box.
31. Q: Why should we be on time?
    A: Being punctual shows responsibility.
32. Q: How can we prepare for the quiz?
    A: By revising the notes and practicing questions.
33. Q: What is the rule for changing tenses?
    A: You must follow the structure for each tense.
34. Q: Who is next for the oral test?
    A: Sanjay is next.
35. Q: When will the new timetable be given?
    A: It will be given on the first day of next term.
36. Q: Where is today's class being held?
    A: In the computer lab.
37. Q: Why are we revising the lesson again?
    A: To help everyone recall and understand better.
38. Q: How should we do the group project?
    A: Divide the work and collaborate as a team.
39. Q: What is the spelling of 'responsibility'?
    A: R-E-S-P-O-N-S-I-B-I-L-I-T-Y.
40. Q: Who is collecting the notebooks today?
    A: Nivedha will collect them.
41. Q: When should we report to the auditorium?
    A: By 9:45 AM.
42. Q: Where will the drawing competition be held?
    A: In the activity hall.
43. Q: Why should we not waste paper?
    A: To protect the environment.
44. Q: How do we greet a visitor to our school?
    A: By saying 'Good Morning' and offering help politely.
45. Q: What should we wear for Sports Day?
    A: White T-shirt and track pants.
46. Q: Who is helping the teacher today?
    A: Arjun and Meena.
47. Q: When will we practice for the skit?
    A: During the 7th period.

48. Q: Where should we place the library books?
    A: On the return shelf.
49. Q: Why is reading important?
    A: It improves language and knowledge.
50. Q: How do we submit the assignment online?
    A: Upload it in the Google Classroom link shared.
51. Q: What is the synonym of 'happy'?
    A: The synonym is 'joyful'.
52. Q: Who wrote this poem?
    A: Rabindranath Tagore wrote it.
53. Q: When is the next English test?
    A: It is on Tuesday next week.
54. Q: Where do we keep our art supplies?
    A: In the cupboard near the window.
55. Q: Why do we do warm-up activities?
    A: To get our minds ready for learning.
56. Q: How do we solve word problems in math?
    A: By identifying keywords and using step-by-step methods.
57. Q: What do you like about the story?
    A: I liked the ending because it was unexpected.
58. Q: Who will help distribute the books?
    A: I will help, ma'am.
59. Q: When is our library due date?
    A: It's this Friday.
60. Q: Where is the science exhibition happening?
    A: In the auditorium.
61. Q: Why should we not talk during class?
    A: It disturbs others and the teacher.
62. Q: How do you use a dictionary?
    A: By looking up the word alphabetically.
63. Q: What do you think the author meant?
    A: I think he meant we should be kind.
64. Q: Who has not completed the project?
    A: I haven't completed it yet, ma'am.
65. Q: When will we get our report cards?
    A: Next Monday.
66. Q: Where can we wash our paintbrushes?
    A: In the sink near the lab.

67. Q: Why do we write essays?

A: To express our ideas clearly and in an organized manner.

68. Q: How can we improve our vocabulary?

A: By reading books and using new words.

69. Q: What is the moral of the story?

A: Honesty is the best policy.

70. Q: Who brought the models for the project?

A: Rahul and Priya brought them.

71. Q: When does the exam begin?

A: At 10 AM.

72. Q: Where is the staff room?

A: On the first floor.

73. Q: Why do we celebrate Environment Day?

A: To raise awareness about protecting nature.

74. Q: How do we conduct a science experiment?

A: By following the steps in the manual carefully.

75. Q: What is your favourite subject?

A: My favourite subject is English.

76. Q: Who is in charge of today's morning prayer?

A: Roshni is, ma'am.

77. Q: When do we leave for the field trip?

A: After the morning assembly.

78. Q: Where do we hang the class chart?

A: Near the entrance door.

79. Q: Why do we recycle materials?

A: To reduce waste and save resources.

80. Q: How can we behave responsibly in class?

A: By following rules and helping each other.

81. Q: What homework do we have today?

A: We have to complete Exercise 3 from the textbook.

82. Q: Who has extra worksheets?

A: I have some extra copies, ma'am.

83. Q: When do we go to the library?

A: Every Thursday during the third period.

84. Q: Where do we find the dictionary section?

A: On the last shelf in the library.

85. Q: Why should we raise hands before speaking?

A: To maintain order and give everyone a chance to speak.

86. Q: How do we conduct a group discussion?

A: By listening, sharing, and taking turns.

87. Q: What is the opposite of 'brave'?

A: The opposite is 'cowardly'.

88. Q: Who is today's class monitor?

A: Vijay is the monitor today.

89. Q: When do we take our lunch break?

A: At 12:30 PM.

90. Q: Where should we keep our school bags?

A: Under the desk neatly.

91. Q: Why are we learning about fractions?

A: Because it is important in daily life and calculations.

92. Q: How can we participate in the essay contest?

A: Submit your entry by Friday to the language teacher.

93. Q: What should we revise for the test?

A: All lessons from Unit 3.

94. Q: Who is our English teacher?

A: R. Rani Sasikala ma'am.

95. Q: When is the next parent-teacher meeting?

A: On the first Saturday of next month.

96. Q: Where can we charge the tablets?

A: In the charging cabinet at the back of the class.

97. Q: Why is teamwork important?

A: Because it helps us achieve common goals efficiently.

98. Q: How do you spell 'achievement'?

A: A-C-H-I-E-V-E-M-E-N-T.

99. Q: What project are we doing this term?

A: A project on local culture and festivals.

100. Q: Who will collect the homework notebooks?

A: Sneha and Arav will collect them.

CHAPTER EIGHT

YES OR NO QUESTIONS

Definition of Yes or No Questions:

A **Yes or No question** is a question that can be answered with a simple "Yes" or "No". It usually begins with an **auxiliary verb** (like *do, does, is, are, can, will,* etc.) or a **modal verb**.

Structure of Yes or No Questions:

1. Present Simple

- **Do** you like apples? → *Yes, I do. / No, I don't.*
- **Does** she play the guitar? → *Yes, she does. / No, she doesn't.*

2. Past Simple

- **Did** they watch the movie? → *Yes, they did. / No, they didn't.*

3. Present Continuous

- **Is** he studying now? → *Yes, he is. / No, he isn't.*
- **Are** you coming with us? → *Yes, I am. / No, I'm not.*

4. Future (will)

- **Will** she attend the meeting? → *Yes, she will. / No, she won't.*

5. Modals

- **Can** you swim? → *Yes, I can. / No, I can't.*
- **Should** I call him now? → *Yes, you should. / No, you shouldn't.*

Yes or No questions

1. Q: Did you complete your homework on time?
A: Yes, I submitted it this morning.
2. Q: Is this your final draft?
A: Yes, I revised it twice.
3. Q: Have you brought your textbook today?
A: No, I forgot to bring it.
4. Q: Is this your notebook?
A: Yes, it has my name on it.
5. Q: Are you ready for the quiz?
A: Yes, I've prepared well.
6. Q: Can you hear me clearly?
A: No, the audio is too low.
7. Q: Do you understand the topic?
A: Yes, it's much clearer now.
8. Q: Did everyone bring their art materials?
A: No, a few students forgot.
9. Q: Is this the correct answer?
A: Yes, it matches the example.
10. Q: Have you submitted your assignment?
A: Yes, I gave it yesterday.
11. Q: Is the class monitor present today?
A: Yes, she is.
12. Q: Are you paying attention?
A: Yes, I'm listening carefully.
13. Q: Have you done the revision?
A: Yes, I revised last night.
14. Q: Is it time to leave for lunch?
A: Yes, the bell just rang.
15. Q: Did you enjoy the story we read?
A: Yes, very much.
16. Q: Do you need help with this question?
A: Yes, please explain it.

17. Q: Is everyone present today?

 A: No, two are absent.

18. Q: Can we start the activity now?

 A: Yes, everything is ready.

19. Q: Do you like working in groups?

 A: Yes, it's more fun.

20. Q: Did you write the date on your notebook?

 A: Yes, at the top.

21. Q: Can you repeat the question?

 A: Yes, I can.

22. Q: Is the board clean?

 A: No, it needs to be wiped.

23. Q: Are you wearing your ID card?

 A: Yes, ma'am.

24. Q: Did you mark your attendance?

 A: No, I forgot.

25. Q: Have you opened your textbook to the right page?

 A: Yes, page 42.

26. Q: Is your name written on the paper?

 A: Yes, at the top.

27. Q: Can we take a short break now?

 A: Yes, after this exercise.

28. Q: Are you feeling unwell?

 A: Yes, a little dizzy.

29. Q: Did you bring your water bottle?

 A: No, I left it at home.

30. Q: Have you learnt the poem by heart?

 A: Yes, I can recite it.

31. Q: Is this the first question of the test?

 A: Yes, it is.

32. Q: Do we have to submit this today?

 A: Yes, before the last period.

33. Q: Can you solve this on the board?

 A: Yes, I'll try.

34. Q: Did the teacher explain the topic yesterday?

 A: Yes, during the second period.

35. Q: Are you working with your partner?

 A: Yes, we're on it.

36. Q: Is this your seat?
 A: No, mine is in the next row.
37. Q: Do you like this activity?
 A: Yes, it's interesting.
38. Q: Have you completed the puzzle?
 A: Yes, in five minutes.
39. Q: Can you hear the audio clearly?
 A: No, it's too faint.
40. Q: Is this answer written in full sentence?
 A: Yes, as required.
41. Q: Are we allowed to use colour pencils?
 A: Yes, for diagrams.
42. Q: Did you participate in the quiz?
 A: Yes, last Friday.
43. Q: Have you visited the library this week?
 A: No, not yet.
44. Q: Is this example helpful?
 A: Yes, very helpful.
45. Q: Do you remember yesterday's lesson?
 A: Yes, we did punctuation.
46. Q: Did the principal visit the class?
 A: Yes, during assembly.
47. Q: Is your handwriting neat?
 A: Yes, I've improved.
48. Q: Are your notes complete?
 A: No, I missed one topic.
49. Q: Can we play a language game today?
 A: Yes, that would be great.
50. Q: Is there a test tomorrow?
 A: Yes, a grammar test.
51. Q: Do you enjoy reading stories?
 A: Yes, especially fiction.
52. Q: Are all group members present?
 A: No, one is absent.
53. Q: Did you understand the homework?
 A: Yes, it was clear.
54. Q: Is the answer written in passive voice?
 A: Yes, correctly.

55. Q: Are you using a pencil for the drawing?
 A: Yes, for neatness.
56. Q: Did you underline the title?
 A: Yes, with a scale.
57. Q: Do we need to write both questions?
 A: Yes, both are compulsory.
58. Q: Can we work on the assignment in pairs?
 A: Yes, it's allowed.
59. Q: Are you attending the special class tomorrow?
 A: Yes, ma'am.
60. Q: Did you practice the poem for recitation?
 A: Yes, yesterday.
61. Q: Have you opened the app for the quiz?
 A: No, not yet.
62. Q: Do you know your roll number?
 A: Yes, it's 18.
63. Q: Is your file organised?
 A: Yes, by subject.
64. Q: Did the bell ring already?
 A: Yes, just now.
65. Q: Are you finished with your work?
 A: No, almost done.
66. Q: Have you corrected your errors?
 A: Yes, I fixed them.
67. Q: Do you need extra time for this task?
 A: Yes, a few minutes.
68. Q: Did your group complete the project?
 A: Yes, last evening.
69. Q: Are you using the same notebook?
 A: Yes, for grammar.
70. Q: Is this your first time presenting?
 A: Yes, I'm nervous.
71. Q: Have you noted down the main points?
 A: Yes, in my notebook.
72. Q: Can you give another example?
 A: Yes, here's one.
73. Q: Are we allowed to discuss now?
 A: No, it's silent reading.

74. Q: Do you think the answer is correct?
 A: Yes, it's accurate.
75. Q: Have you taken your seat?
 A: Yes, ma'am.
76. Q: Did you use a blue pen?
 A: No, I used black.
77. Q: Are your diagrams labelled?
 A: Yes, clearly.
78. Q: Is there any doubt in this topic?
 A: No, it's clear.
79. Q: Can you explain your answer?
 A: Yes, with the rule.
80. Q: Did you follow the format?
 A: Yes, for both questions.
81. Q: Have you shared the worksheet with your partner?
 A: Yes, we're working together.
82. Q: Is the chart ready for display?
 A: Yes, on the board.
83. Q: Are your materials ready for the activity?
 A: Yes, all packed.
84. Q: Did you take part in the role-play?
 A: Yes, I was the narrator.
85. Q: Have you prepared for tomorrow's speech?
 A: Yes, I memorised it.
86. Q: Do you want to ask a question?
 A: Yes, about the rule.
87. Q: Is the textbook interesting?
 A: Yes, it has great stories.
88. Q: Are your group members cooperating?
 A: Yes, we're helping.
89. Q: Can we revise together in groups?
 A: Yes, after the class.
90. Q: Did you copy the notes correctly?
 A: Yes, from the board.
91. Q: Is the internet working?
 A: No, it's slow.
92. Q: Have you drawn the table in your notebook?
 A: Yes, neatly.

93. Q: Are you confident for the test?

 A: Yes, I studied well.

94. Q: Did the teacher give feedback?

 A: Yes, on the assignment.

95. Q: Do you need another sheet?

 A: Yes, mine is full.

96. Q: Is this the final draft?

 A: No, still revising.

97. Q: Have you reviewed the rules?

 A: Yes, during the last class.

98. Q: Are you going to submit it now?

 A: Yes, it's ready.

99. Q: Did you enjoy the activity?

 A: Yes, very much.

100. Q: Is this sentence grammatically correct?

 A: No, it lacks a verb.

101. Q: Have you completed the reading task?

 A: Yes, I finished it last night.

102. Q: Do you want to read aloud next?

 A: Yes, I'd love to.

103. Q: Is the title of your essay underlined?

 A: Yes, with a scale.

104. Q: Have you checked your spellings?

 A: Yes, I used a dictionary.

105. Q: Can you draw the diagram on the board?

 A: Yes, I can.

106. Q: Is your project file colourful and creative?

 A: Yes, I used pictures and headings.

107. Q: Did you work on the correction sheet?

 A: Yes, I corrected all the errors.

108. Q: Do you want more examples for practice?

 A: Yes, that would help.

109. Q: Have you memorised the new vocabulary?

 A: Yes, I practised them last night.

110. Q: Are your group members sharing tasks?

 A: Yes, we divided the work equally.

111. Q: Did the teacher appreciate your effort?

 A: Yes, she praised my presentation.

112. Q: Have you pasted the chart in your notebook?

A: No, I'll do it today.

113. Q: Can we revise yesterday's topic once more?

A: Yes, please.

114. Q: Are you writing the answers in full sentences?

A: Yes, as instructed.

115. Q: Do you have a question about this topic?

A: No, it's clear now.

116. Q: Is your compass box complete?

A: Yes, it has all the tools.

117. Q: Did you check the answer key?

A: Yes, I matched my answers.

118. Q: Have you written the summary in your own words?

A: Yes, I didn't copy it.

119. Q: Is your handwriting legible?

A: Yes, I made it neat.

120. Q: Did you attend the reading session?

A: No, I was absent.

121. Q: Are your worksheets arranged in order?

A: Yes, by date.

122. Q: Have you answered all the questions?

A: Yes, none are left.

123. Q: Can we revise this poem again?

A: Yes, one more time would help.

124. Q: Is your paper double-sided?

A: No, I used only one side.

125. Q: Did you draw the margins on your page?

A: Yes, with a ruler.

126. Q: Are your class notes up to date?

A: Yes, I completed them last night.

127. Q: Have you signed the permission slip?

A: No, I forgot.

128. Q: Is your school bag packed for tomorrow?

A: Yes, I checked everything.

129. Q: Did you complete the comprehension passage?

A: Yes, I answered all the questions.

130. Q: Are you confident in solving these sums?

A: Yes, I practised them well.

131. Q: Have you written the correct date?
A: Yes, today's date.

132. Q: Do you need help with pronunciation?
A: Yes, for a few words.

133. Q: Is this your handwriting on the board?
A: Yes, I wrote it during the activity.

134. Q: Did you complete the paragraph writing task?
A: No, I'm still writing.

135. Q: Have you pasted the worksheet in your notebook?
A: Yes, neatly.

136. Q: Do you need another notebook?
A: Yes, this one is full.

137. Q: Is the sentence written in direct speech?
A: Yes, with quotation marks.

138. Q: Did you write the correct answer in the blank?
A: Yes, I checked it twice.

139. Q: Are you ready with your script for the skit?
A: Yes, we practised it together.

140. Q: Have you chosen your topic for the project?
A: Yes, it's about solar energy.

141. Q: Did you stick the diagram in the notebook?
A: Yes, with glue.

142. Q: Are you sitting in your assigned place?
A: Yes, ma'am.

143. Q: Do you want to share your idea with the class?
A: Yes, I have something to say.

144. Q: Have you checked the spelling of this word?
A: Yes, I used a dictionary.

145. Q: Is your answer similar to the example given?
A: Yes, it follows the same pattern.

146. Q: Did you follow the time limit for the task?
A: No, I needed extra time.

147. Q: Are you prepared for the oral assessment?
A: Yes, I revised all the topics.

148. Q: Did you enjoy today's class?
A: Yes, it was very interactive.

149. Q: Did you follow the instructions carefully?
A: Yes, I followed every step.

150. Q: Are your assignments submitted on time?
  A: Yes, I always submit them early.
151. Q: Have you highlighted the key points?
  A: Yes, using a yellow marker.
152. Q: Did you use a ruler to draw the table?
  A: Yes, for straight lines.
153. Q: Is the topic clear to you now?
  A: Yes, I understand it better.
154. Q: Do you need help with this exercise?
  A: No, I can manage it myself.
155. Q: Have you checked your answers?
  A: Yes, I revised them twice.
156. Q: Is this a group task?
  A: Yes, we are doing it together.
157. Q: Did you get full marks in spelling?
  A: Yes, I got 10 out of 10.
158. Q: Are your books covered and labelled?
  A: Yes, with name and subject.
159. Q: Did you practise the conversation at home?
  A: Yes, I practised with my sister.
160. Q: Are you ready to write the summary?
  A: Yes, I've made notes already.
161. Q: Have you prepared your speech draft?
  A: No, I'm still working on it.
162. Q: Did the teacher check your notebook?
  A: Yes, yesterday during class.
163. Q: Is the heading written in capital letters?
  A: Yes, it is.
164. Q: Do you want more time to complete this?
  A: Yes, five more minutes please.
165. Q: Have you chosen your library book?
  A: Yes, I picked a mystery novel.
166. Q: Are you waiting for your turn?
  A: Yes, I'll go next.
167. Q: Did you bring your painting supplies?
  A: No, I forgot my brushes.
168. Q: Is your paragraph within the word limit?
  A: Yes, it's exactly 80 words.

169. Q: Did you edit your rough draft?
  A: Yes, I made the corrections.
170. Q: Are you following the teacher's explanation?
  A: Yes, I'm noting it down too.
171. Q: Have you saved your file properly?
  A: Yes, it's in the class folder.
172. Q: Do you need help logging in?
  A: No, I remember the password.
173. Q: Is the map coloured correctly?
  A: Yes, I used the right shades.
174. Q: Have you joined the online class?
  A: Yes, I'm already logged in.
175. Q: Did you watch the educational video?
  A: Yes, it was interesting.
176. Q: Are your corrections clearly marked?
  A: Yes, I used a red pen.
177. Q: Did you take notes during the lecture?
  A: Yes, I wrote the main points.
178. Q: Is your answer sheet neat and clean?
  A: Yes, no overwriting.
179. Q: Do you want to answer the next question?
  A: Yes, ma'am.
180. Q: Have you updated your assignment list?
  A: Yes, I added today's task.
181. Q: Are you ready to explain your answer?
  A: Yes, I can explain it now.
182. Q: Did you use all the vocabulary words?
  A: Yes, in different sentences.
183. Q: Is this a complete sentence?
  A: No, it's missing a subject.
184. Q: Have you labelled the diagram correctly?
  A: Yes, all parts are marked.
185. Q: Did the teacher correct your grammar?
  A: Yes, she underlined the errors.
186. Q: Are you prepared for the dictation?
  A: Yes, I revised the spelling list.
187. Q: Do you need help choosing a topic?
  A: No, I've already decided.

188. Q: Have you filled in all the blanks?

A: Yes, I answered each one.

189. Q: Did you write the title in bold?

A: Yes, using a black pen.

190. Q: Is your handwriting consistent?

A: Yes, throughout the page.

191. Q: Are your answers in the correct order?

A: Yes, as per the question numbers.

192. Q: Did you include a conclusion in your essay?

A: Yes, I wrote the final paragraph.

193. Q: Have you revised yesterday's lesson?

A: Yes, before coming to school.

194. Q: Is this an even number?

A: Yes, it is divisible by 2.

195. Q: Did you work silently during the activity?

A: Yes, without any disturbance.

196. Q: Are you able to follow the online class?

A: Yes, the audio is clear.

197. Q: Do you want to change your topic?

A: No, I'm happy with it.

198. Q: Have you written your name on the test paper?

A: Yes, on the top right corner.

199. Q: Did you follow the paragraph structure?

A: Yes, I started with a topic sentence.

200. Q: Is your assignment based on the correct topic?

A: Yes, I confirmed it before writing.

201. Q: Have you practised the dialogue with your partner?

A: Yes, we rehearsed twice.

202. Q: Are your answers supported with examples?

A: Yes, I added two examples.

203. Q: Did you complete the online quiz?

A: Yes, I submitted it on time.

204. Q: Is your table aligned properly in the notebook?

A: Yes, I used the margins.

205. Q: Have you corrected the spelling mistakes?

A: Yes, using the teacher's feedback.

206. Q: Do you want to read the poem aloud?

A: Yes, I would love to.

207. Q: Are your materials arranged neatly?
A: Yes, all are in order.

208. Q: Did you take part in the debate competition?
A: Yes, I spoke for the motion.

209. Q: Have you uploaded the assignment on the portal?
A: Yes, I uploaded it yesterday.

210. Q: Is this diagram part of your science project?
A: Yes, it explains the life cycle.

211. Q: Did you share your notes with your classmate?
A: Yes, through the class group.

212. Q: Have you revised the previous lesson?
A: Yes, before class started.

213. Q: Is this topic covered in the syllabus?
A: Yes, it's part of Unit 4.

214. Q: Do you need clarification on the topic?
A: No, I understood it.

215. Q: Have you listed the main characters?
A: Yes, all of them.

216. Q: Is your speech within the time limit?
A: Yes, under 2 minutes.

217. Q: Did you draw the conclusion in your report?
A: Yes, it's in the last paragraph.

218. Q: Are your grammar notes complete?
A: Yes, from all three chapters.

219. Q: Have you joined the Google Classroom?
A: Yes, with the code shared.

220. Q: Is the chart related to environmental studies?
A: Yes, it shows water conservation methods.

221. Q: Did you attend the workshop yesterday?
A: No, I was absent.

222. Q: Are you carrying your reading log?
A: Yes, it's in my bag.

223. Q: Have you prepared your part for the skit?
A: Yes, I memorised it.

224. Q: Do you enjoy project-based learning?
A: Yes, it's very engaging.

225. Q: Is your answer sheet signed by the teacher?
A: Yes, after correction.

226. Q: Did you complete the crossword puzzle?
  A: Yes, it was fun.
227. Q: Have you done peer correction today?
  A: Yes, we swapped notebooks.
228. Q: Are you ready for the surprise test?
  A: Yes, I studied last night.
229. Q: Did the teacher explain the new topic today?
  A: Yes, during the first period.
230. Q: Is this your first draft or final?
  A: It's the final version.
231. Q: Have you checked the marking scheme?
  A: Yes, it's on the notice board.
232. Q: Did you use colour in your chart?
  A: Yes, for better presentation.
233. Q: Do you prefer group discussions?
  A: Yes, I learn a lot from peers.
234. Q: Have you practised your lines for the play?
  A: Yes, I know them by heart.
235. Q: Is this your personal opinion?
  A: Yes, based on my experience.
236. Q: Did you watch the documentary assigned?
  A: No, I missed it.
237. Q: Are you prepared to explain your project?
  A: Yes, I made cue cards.
238. Q: Have you included a title for your poster?
  A: Yes, it's bold and centered.
239. Q: Is the worksheet attached to your notebook?
  A: Yes, I glued it in.
240. Q: Did you work with your team on the chart?
  A: Yes, we divided the work.
241. Q: Have you listed the objectives of your topic?
  A: Yes, at the beginning.
242. Q: Is the summary written in your own words?
  A: Yes, I avoided copying.
243. Q: Do you need help to present your topic?
  A: No, I can manage.
244. Q: Have you written the bibliography?
  A: Yes, at the end of the report.

245. Q: Is your homework checked by the teacher?
A: Yes, she returned it today.

246. Q: Did you answer all the comprehension questions?
A: Yes, even the extra one.

247. Q: Have you marked important points while reading?
A: Yes, with a pencil.

248. Q: Do you enjoy working on educational apps?
A: Yes, they make learning fun.

249. Q: Is your project displayed on the wall?
A: Yes, near the entrance.

250. Q: Did you give a speech on assembly day?
A: Yes, on Independence Day.

251. Q: Have you submitted your journal?
A: Yes, it's with the teacher.

252. Q: Did you organize your study materials?
A: Yes, in separate folders.

253. Q: Have you written the reflection paragraph?
A: Yes, it's at the end.

254. Q: Is the assignment based on a real story?
A: Yes, it's a biography.

255. Q: Did your group present on time?
A: Yes, we were the first.

256. Q: Are the charts laminated?
A: Yes, to preserve them.

257. Q: Have you created a presentation slide?
A: Yes, using PowerPoint.

258. Q: Is the reading corner updated?
A: Yes, with new books.

259. Q: Did the librarian help you find the book?
A: Yes, she guided me.

260. Q: Have you practiced using punctuation marks?
A: Yes, with examples.

261. Q: Do you enjoy watching historical films?
A: Yes, they are informative.

262. Q: Have you taken part in a science exhibition?
A: Yes, last semester.

263. Q: Is your notebook divided by subject?
A: Yes, with labeled sections.

264. Q: Did you download the study materials?

    A: Yes, from the portal.

265. Q: Have you used a graphic organizer?

    A: Yes, for summarizing.

266. Q: Did you ask a question during the webinar?

    A: Yes, about grammar.

267. Q: Have you created a mind map?

    A: Yes, on the poem.

268. Q: Did you revise for the vocabulary test?

    A: Yes, I used flashcards.

269. Q: Is this poem written in rhyming couplets?

    A: Yes, it follows that pattern.

270. Q: Have you bookmarked the practice exercises?

    A: Yes, all links saved.

271. Q: Did you decorate the project file?

    A: Yes, with stickers and borders.

272. Q: Have you explained the plot diagram?

    A: Yes, using a chart.

273. Q: Do you follow the reading schedule?

    A: Yes, every evening.

274. Q: Have you added a glossary to your project?

    A: Yes, on the last page.

275. Q: Did the guest speaker interact with students?

    A: Yes, it was engaging.

276. Q: Have you checked the project rubric?

    A: Yes, before submitting.

277. Q: Is your introduction paragraph catchy?

    A: Yes, it starts with a question.

278. Q: Have you cited your sources?

    A: Yes, in MLA format.

279. Q: Did the teacher approve your topic?

    A: Yes, during consultation.

280. Q: Have you included transition words?

    A: Yes, in each paragraph.

281. Q: Is your conclusion well-summarized?

    A: Yes, it wraps up the idea.

282. Q: Did you add captions to your images?

    A: Yes, under each one.

283. Q: Have you proofread your final draft?

A: Yes, before printing.

284. Q: Is this activity based on experiential learning?

A: Yes, it includes hands-on tasks.

285. Q: Did you submit the peer review form?

A: Yes, I reviewed my partner's work.

286. Q: Have you joined the English club?

A: Yes, I signed up yesterday.

287. Q: Is your assignment handwritten or typed?

A: Typed, as per instructions.

288. Q: Did you create a timeline for the story?

A: Yes, with key events.

289. Q: Have you written a character sketch?

A: Yes, for the main character.

290. Q: Did you annotate the text?

A: Yes, with notes and symbols.

291. Q: Is the classroom library open daily?

A: Yes, during lunch break.

292. Q: Have you joined the reading challenge?

A: Yes, I started last week.

293. Q: Did the teacher assign you a role?

A: Yes, I'm the team leader.

294. Q: Have you drawn the character map?

A: Yes, for all key roles.

295. Q: Is your learning log updated?

A: Yes, till this week.

296. Q: Did you set a reading goal?

A: Yes, two books a month.

297. Q: Have you written a book review?

A: Yes, for the novel we read.

298. Q: Is your article ready for the school magazine?

A: Yes, it's been edited.

299. Q: Have you participated in the reading circle?

A: Yes, I read chapter four.

300. Q: Did the teacher record your speaking test?

A: Yes, for feedback.

301. Q: Have you received your graded rubric?

A: Yes, yesterday.

302. Q: Did you watch the play adaptation?
  A: Yes, on the school projector.
303. Q: Have you drafted your letter to the editor?
  A: Yes, about school facilities.
304. Q: Is your portfolio complete?
  A: Yes, with all components.
305. Q: Did you attend the storytelling session?
  A: Yes, it was fun.
306. Q: Have you presented your travelogue?
  A: Yes, last week.
307. Q: Is your comprehension sheet marked?
  A: Yes, with remarks.
308. Q: Did your team win the reading contest?
  A: Yes, we got first place.
309. Q: Have you participated in an elocution contest?
  A: Yes, in Grade 8.
310. Q: Did you upload your assignment on time?
  A: Yes, before the deadline.
311. Q: Is your title page decorated?
  A: Yes, with borders and color.
312. Q: Have you practiced tongue twisters?
  A: Yes, for pronunciation.
313. Q: Did the teacher assign a peer evaluator?
  A: Yes, I have one.
314. Q: Have you added a cover page to your report?
  A: Yes, with my details.
315. Q: Is this article written in the third person?
  A: Yes, it avoids 'I'.
316. Q: Have you discussed your topic with the teacher?
  A: Yes, during consultation hours.
317. Q: Did the classroom discussion help you understand?
  A: Yes, it clarified many doubts.
318. Q: Have you rehearsed your welcome speech?
  A: Yes, three times.
319. Q: Is your homework pinned on the board?
  A: Yes, as the best entry.
320. Q: Did you present your biography project?
  A: Yes, on Wednesday.

321. Q: Have you added feedback notes to your journal?
A: Yes, after every task.

322. Q: Is the poem written with metaphors?
A: Yes, it uses several.

323. Q: Have you analysed the main theme?
A: Yes, it's clearly outlined.

324. Q: Did you add references to the back matter?
A: Yes, under 'Sources'.

325. Q: Have you organised a reading session before?
A: Yes, in last term.

326. Q: Is the rubric attached to your work?
A: Yes, on the last page.

327. Q: Did you use storytelling in your oral test?
A: Yes, to explain the plot.

328. Q: Have you made flashcards for revision?
A: Yes, with key points.

329. Q: Is your outline submitted for approval?
A: Yes, it was accepted.

330. Q: Have you formatted the document correctly?
A: Yes, with headings and margins.

331. Q: Did you peer edit a friend's draft?
A: Yes, last night.

332. Q: Is your skit based on a moral lesson?
A: Yes, it teaches honesty.

333. Q: Have you colour-coded your notes?
A: Yes, using markers.

334. Q: Did the teacher ask you to revise the draft?
A: Yes, I'm revising it.

335. Q: Have you written a dialogue-based script?
A: Yes, for the play.

336. Q: Did you explore the central conflict of the story?
A: Yes, in detail.

337. Q: Have you aligned the content to the learning outcome?
A: Yes, it matches perfectly.

338. Q: Is the classroom blog updated weekly?
A: Yes, by our monitor.

339. Q: Did your group lead the morning assembly?
A: Yes, this Monday.

340. Q: Have you included a thank-you note?
A: Yes, at the end.

341. Q: Is your assignment based on a news report?
A: Yes, from The Hindu.

342. Q: Did you listen to the audio task?
A: Yes, and completed it.

343. Q: Have you recorded your narration?
A: Yes, using the class app.

344. Q: Is the lesson plan printed?
A: Yes, in A4 size.

345. Q: Did you revise the editing checklist?
A: Yes, all items marked.

346. Q: Have you submitted your activity log?
A: Yes, every week.

347. Q: Did you prepare questions for the author talk?
A: Yes, three thoughtful ones.

348. Q: Have you quoted examples from the text?
A: Yes, in each answer.

349. Q: Is your bookmark project completed?
A: Yes, and laminated.

350. Q: Did you get parent signature on your project?
A: Yes, on the last page.

351. Q: Have you received your participation certificate?
A: Yes, from the headmistress.

352. Q: Is your class display board up to date?
A: Yes, with new entries.

353. Q: Did your summary include the main points?
A: Yes, all covered.

354. Q: Have you worked on language enrichment tasks?
A: Yes, this week's set.

355. Q: Is this report a comparative analysis?
A: Yes, between two poems.

356. Q: Did you label each part of the project?
A: Yes, with tags.

357. Q: Have you included a fun fact section?
A: Yes, on the side panel.

358. Q: Did you explore symbolism in the story?
A: Yes, especially with objects.

359. Q: Have you discussed the narrative voice?
A: Yes, in the review.

360. Q: Did you follow the newspaper format?
A: Yes, for the layout.

361. Q: Have you maintained the reading journal?
A: Yes, with weekly updates.

362. Q: Is the task rubric explained clearly?
A: Yes, in class.

363. Q: Did your visual aid enhance understanding?
A: Yes, the diagram helped.

364. Q: Have you watched the educational animation?
A: Yes, on solar energy.

365. Q: Did the English lab session help you?
A: Yes, it was interactive.

366. Q: Have you written a plot summary?
A: Yes, within 100 words.

367. Q: Is your skit script original?
A: Yes, we created it.

368. Q: Have you illustrated the story book?
A: Yes, with hand drawings.

369. Q: Did the group complete the role play?
A: Yes, during last period.

370. Q: Have you translated the passage?
A: Yes, into Tamil.

371. Q: Is the assignment submitted via Google Classroom?
A: Yes, as a PDF.

372. Q: Did the vocabulary quiz include synonyms?
A: Yes, ten of them.

373. Q: Have you completed the draft worksheet?
A: Yes, all questions done.

374. Q: Did you insert headings in your essay?
A: Yes, for each part.

375. Q: Have you designed a title banner?
A: Yes, for our wall magazine.

376. Q: Did you correct your spelling errors?
A: Yes, using the dictionary.

377. Q: Have you included transition phrases?
A: Yes, like "on the other hand".

378. Q: Is this assignment a group project?

A: Yes, with four members.

379. Q: Did the teacher show a sample draft?

A: Yes, for our reference.

380. Q: Have you printed the bibliography page?

A: Yes, on separate sheet.

381. Q: Did you work on vocabulary enhancement?

A: Yes, five new words.

382. Q: Have you reflected on your learning?

A: Yes, in the final paragraph.

383. Q: Is the poem analysis done in pairs?

A: Yes, I worked with Arya.

384. Q: Did the team receive appreciation?

A: Yes, for creativity.

385. Q: Have you completed all five tasks?

A: Yes, in the workbook.

386. Q: Did the literary fest include your entry?

A: Yes, my poem was selected.

387. Q: Have you set personal goals in the journal?

A: Yes, for speaking skills.

388. Q: Is the story map neat and accurate?

A: Yes, all parts included.

389. Q: Did your chart include the citation?

A: Yes, at the bottom.

390. Q: Have you made corrections using red pen?

A: Yes, as instructed.

391. Q: Did you scan the QR code for content?

A: Yes, it worked fine.

392. Q: Have you joined the poem recitation team?

A: Yes, for the finals.

393. Q: Is your theme supported with examples?

A: Yes, from real life.

394. Q: Did the teacher assign a word limit?

A: Yes, 200 words.

395. Q: Have you completed your self-assessment?

A: Yes, with remarks.

396. Q: Did the teacher ask for a creative ending?

A: Yes, I added one.

397. Q: Is your essay written in paragraphs?
A: Yes, with indentations.

398. Q: Have you used similes in your description?
A: Yes, at least three.

399. Q: Did you proofread for punctuation errors?
A: Yes, and corrected them.

400. Q: Have you updated your grammar tracker?
A: Yes, till today.

401. Q: Is the tone of your writing formal?
A: Yes, as per rubric.

402. Q: Did you create a dialogue journal?
A: Yes, for peer exchange.

403. Q: Have you aligned the font as required?
A: Yes, Times New Roman.

404. Q: Is your draft submitted before the deadline?
A: Yes, one day early.

405. Q: Did the teacher give individual feedback?
A: Yes, through the portal.

406. Q: Have you edited your project introduction?
A: Yes, it's more concise now.

407. Q: Did the class discuss different text genres?
A: Yes, in the last session.

408. Q: Have you organized your digital folder?
A: Yes, by topic and date.

409. Q: Is your title relevant to the content?
A: Yes, it reflects the theme.

410. Q: Have you explored character motivation?
A: Yes, especially for the protagonist.

411. Q: Did you complete the peer assessment form?
A: Yes, and shared it.

412. Q: Have you updated your presentation slides?
A: Yes, with better visuals.

413. Q: Is the question framed in active voice?
A: Yes, it's direct and clear.

414. Q: Did your group complete the comic strip?
A: Yes, it's on the board.

415. Q: Have you printed your speech draft?
A: Yes, for the teacher to review.

416. Q: Is your summary structured in three parts?
  A: Yes, beginning, middle, end.
417. Q: Have you revised the idioms list?
  A: Yes, I remember most of them.
418. Q: Did the class conduct a debate last week?
  A: Yes, on environmental issues.
419. Q: Have you submitted your review reflection?
  A: Yes, in the journal.
420. Q: Is the sentence grammatically complex?
  A: Yes, with subordinate clauses.
421. Q: Have you added quotes from the story?
  A: Yes, with page numbers.
422. Q: Did the teacher use a rubric for grading?
  A: Yes, it was shared.
423. Q: Have you uploaded your final version?
  A: Yes, before midnight.
424. Q: Did you read the author background section?
  A: Yes, very informative.
425. Q: Have you rewritten the opening paragraph?
  A: Yes, to make it stronger.
426. Q: Did you draw your interpretation of the poem?
  A: Yes, with color.
427. Q: Have you submitted your extended essay?
  A: Yes, it's uploaded.
428. Q: Is your assignment aligned to the topic?
  A: Yes, clearly linked.
429. Q: Have you corrected the sentence structure?
  A: Yes, using class notes.
430. Q: Did the teacher distribute sample answers?
  A: Yes, for comparison.
431. Q: Have you identified the main conflict?
  A: Yes, it's internal.
432. Q: Did you add a table of contents?
  A: Yes, on the first page.
433. Q: Have you proofread your annotations?
  A: Yes, twice.
434. Q: Is the thesis statement in your introduction?
  A: Yes, clearly stated.

435. Q: Have you added figurative language examples?
A: Yes, two in each stanza.

436. Q: Did the teacher explain the marking scheme?
A: Yes, in yesterday's class.

437. Q: Have you completed the assigned reading?
A: Yes, all chapters.

438. Q: Is your script free of spelling mistakes?
A: Yes, I double-checked.

439. Q: Did the class present visual projects?
A: Yes, last Friday.

440. Q: Have you noted down unfamiliar words?
A: Yes, in a glossary.

441. Q: Did you meet the word count requirement?
A: Yes, 250 words exactly.

442. Q: Have you applied correct tenses?
A: Yes, throughout.

443. Q: Is your draft file saved with your name?
A: Yes, as instructed.

444. Q: Have you labeled the essay sections?
A: Yes, clearly marked.

445. Q: Did the teacher provide prompt choices?
A: Yes, three of them.

446. Q: Have you worked on improving coherence?
A: Yes, using transitions.

447. Q: Is the writing assignment double-spaced?
A: Yes, as per guidelines.

448. Q: Did the teacher give sample thesis ideas?
A: Yes, five were shared.

449. Q: Have you uploaded the audio recording?
A: Yes, through the portal.

450. Q: Did you write a metaphor for your title?
A: Yes, it's symbolic.

451. Q: Have you submitted the final checklist?
A: Yes, with tick marks.

452. Q: Is your written task printed on A4 paper?
A: Yes, single-sided.

453. Q: Did you draw visual elements for the essay?
A: Yes, to support ideas.

454. Q: Have you reflected on peer comments?
 A: Yes, I revised accordingly.

455. Q: Did you record your poetry reading?
 A: Yes, in MP3 format.

456. Q: Have you signed the assignment submission sheet?
 A: Yes, this morning.

457. Q: Did you draft a paragraph using connectors?
 A: Yes, for fluency.

458. Q: Have you highlighted important quotations?
 A: Yes, in yellow.

459. Q: Is your report edited for passive voice?
 A: Yes, where needed.

460. Q: Did you complete the reflection worksheet?
 A: Yes, in the last period.

461. Q: Have you written the author's purpose?
 A: Yes, in the margin.

462. Q: Did the class receive feedback as a group?
 A: Yes, during circle time.

463. Q: Have you backed up your file online?
 A: Yes, in Google Drive.

464. Q: Did you include a dedication in your project?
 A: Yes, to my mentor.

465. Q: Is your article published on the school blog?
 A: Yes, this week.

466. Q: Have you completed your theme-based paragraph?
 A: Yes, in the last page.

467. Q: Did the teacher return the graded rubric?
 A: Yes, yesterday.

468. Q: Have you labeled the graph in your report?
 A: Yes, with units.

469. Q: Did you time your oral presentation?
 A: Yes, it's under 3 minutes.

470. Q: Have you sorted your notes by date?
 A: Yes, in order.

471. Q: Is your character analysis in bullet points?
 A: Yes, for clarity.

472. Q: Did the teacher suggest any changes?
 A: Yes, to the conclusion.

473. Q: Have you recorded the interview answers?
A: Yes, on my phone.

474. Q: Did you proofread your reflection log?
A: Yes, it's clean now.

475. Q: Have you revised your topic sentence?
A: Yes, it's more direct.

476. Q: Is your work saved in PDF format?
A: Yes, as required.

477. Q: Have you signed the peer feedback form?
A: Yes, after reading.

478. Q: Did you receive an extension deadline?
A: Yes, due to illness.

479. Q: Have you written a persuasive conclusion?
A: Yes, with strong points.

480. Q: Did your article follow the headline format?
A: Yes, as shown in class.

481. Q: Have you included an attention grabber?
A: Yes, in the opening line.

482. Q: Is your visual aid colored and labeled?
A: Yes, neatly.

483. Q: Did the teacher display your paragraph?
A: Yes, on the notice board.

484. Q: Have you rewritten the middle paragraph?
A: Yes, to improve clarity.

485. Q: Did you set reminders for assignment deadlines?
A: Yes, on my phone.

486. Q: Have you marked key literary devices?
A: Yes, using underlines.

487. Q: Is your poem typed and centered?
A: Yes, on the page.

488. Q: Have you paraphrased the summary section?
A: Yes, in simple words.

489. Q: Did the teacher provide audio feedback?
A: Yes, via the app.

490. Q: Have you formatted the citations correctly?
A: Yes, using MLA.

491. Q: Did your story have a surprise ending?
A: Yes, it shocked everyone.

492. Q: Have you selected a poem for memorization?

A: Yes, by Robert Frost.

493. Q: Is your submission uploaded to the folder?

A: Yes, in the class drive.

494. Q: Did you organize your thoughts with a mind map?

A: Yes, before writing.

495. Q: Have you submitted the task reflection?

A: Yes, with honest input.

496. Q: Did you include a personal opinion paragraph?

A: Yes, in the conclusion.

497. Q: Have you identified three poetic devices?

A: Yes, with examples.

498. Q: Is your paragraph rich in vocabulary?

A: Yes, with descriptive words.

499. Q: Did the teacher discuss rubric changes?

A: Yes, during the session.

500. Q: Have you printed a clean copy for submission?

A: Yes, no errors.

CHAPTER NINE

CONTRACTIONS IN ENGLISH

Full Form → Contraction

I am → I'm
You are → You're
He is → He's
She is → She's
It is → It's
We are → We're
They are → They're
That is → That's
There is → There's
Who is → Who's
What is → What's
Where is → Where's
When is → When's
Why is → Why's
How is → How's
I have → I've
You have → You've
We have → We've
They have → They've
He has → He's
She has → She's

It has → It's
Could have → Could've
Would have → Would've
Should have → Should've
Might have → Might've
Must have → Must've
I will → I'll
You will → You'll
He will → He'll
She will → She'll
It will → It'll
We will → We'll
They will → They'll
I would → I'd
You would → You'd
He would → He'd
She would → She'd
It would → It'd
We would → We'd
They would → They'd
I had → I'd
You had → You'd
He had → He'd
She had → She'd
It had → It'd
We had → We'd
They had → They'd
Is not → Isn't
Are not → Aren't
Was not → Wasn't
Were not → Weren't
Have not → Haven't
Has not → Hasn't
Had not → Hadn't
Will not → Won't
Would not → Wouldn't

Should not → Shouldn't
Could not → Couldn't
Might not → Mightn't
Must not → Mustn't
Do not → Don't
Does not → Doesn't
Did not → Didn't
Cannot → Can't
Need not → Needn't
Ought not → Oughtn't
Let us → Let's
Give me → Gimme
Tell them → Tell'em
Going to → Gonna
Want to → Wanna
Got to → Gotta
What are you → Whatcha
Don't you → Don'tcha
Would you → Wouldja
Could you → Couldja
Did you → Didja
You all → Y'all
Am not / Is not / Are not → Ain't
Madam → Ma'am
It is → 'Tis
It was → 'Twas
Come on → C'mon
You know → Y'know
Because → 'Cause
I am going to → I'mma
Let me → Lemme
Do not know → Dunno
Should have → Shoulda
Could have → Coulda
Would have → Woulda
I am going to → Ima

Out of → Outta
Lot of → Lotta
Kind of → Kinda
Sort of → Sorta
All right → Alright
Would not have → Wouldn't've
They would have → They'd've

CHAPTER TEN

CONVERSATION WITH COLLEAGUES

I. Sample conversation inside the staffroom

1. Casual Conversation in the Staff Room

Ms. Priya: Good morning, Mr. Ramesh!

Mr. Ramesh: Good morning, Priya! How was your English class today?

Ms. Priya: It went well. We were discussing essay writing techniques. The students were quite engaged.

Mr. Ramesh: That's great. I find writing sessions a bit challenging to manage.

Ms. Priya: True, but once they get the structure, it becomes easier. How about your science class?

Mr. Ramesh: We did an experiment today. The kids were excited to see the chemical reaction.

Ms. Priya: Practical activities always bring the lesson to life.

2. Planning a School Event

Ms. Latha: Hello, Mr. Arun. Are you free for a quick discussion about the Annual Day program?

Mr. Arun: Yes, of course. What do we need to plan?

Ms. Latha: We need to finalise the student performances. I'm handling the skit, and I think we could use your help with the music selection.

Mr. Arun: Sure, I can help with that. I'll also ask the music teacher to guide the students.

Ms. Latha: Perfect. Let's schedule a rehearsal next Friday?

Mr. Arun: That works. I'll inform the students and prepare the audio system.

3. Discussing a Student's Performance

Ms. Rekha: Hi, Mr. Suresh. I wanted to talk about Rahul from Class 9.

Mr. Suresh: Yes, I've noticed he's been very quiet lately.

Ms. Rekha: He's not submitting assignments in my class. Is it the same in yours?

Mr. Suresh: Yes, and he seems distracted. Maybe we should call his parents for a meeting.

Ms. Rekha: Agreed. It's better to address it early. I'll coordinate with the class teacher.

4. After a Staff Meeting

Mr. Vinod: That was quite a long meeting!

Ms. Deepa: Yes, but important. The changes in the exam pattern will require some adjustment.

Mr. Vinod: Especially the introduction of the competency-based questions.

Ms. Deepa: We should plan a workshop for teachers next week to handle it.

Mr. Vinod: Good idea. I'll speak to the principal about it.

5. Talking About a Substitute Teacher

Ms. Anjali: Hello, Mr. Kiran. I heard you were absent yesterday.

Mr. Kiran: Yes, I wasn't well. Thanks for informing the class.

Ms. Anjali: No problem. I arranged a substitute for your 10A math class.

Mr. Kiran: I appreciate it. I'll check their notebooks today and give some revision tomorrow.

Ms. Anjali: Good idea. They did mention the sub was a bit strict!

Mr. Kiran: Sometimes, that helps keep them in line!

6. Preparing for a Parent-Teacher Meeting

Mr. Joseph: Are you ready for the parent-teacher meeting tomorrow?

Ms. Fathima: Almost. I just need to update my student progress sheets.

Mr. Joseph: I prepared a summary for each student – makes the conversation easier.

Ms. Fathima: That's smart. I'll do that tonight. I'm expecting a few tough questions.

Mr. Joseph: Just stay calm and be honest. Most parents just want to help their children.

7. Coordinating Exam Duties

Ms. Seema: Mr. Raj, are you on exam duty tomorrow morning?

Mr. Raj: Yes, I'm assigned to Room 5 from 9 a.m.

Ms. Seema: I'm in Room 6. Let's coordinate the entry time and bell ringing.

Mr. Raj: Sure. We should be at the exam hall by 8:45 to set up.

Ms. Seema: And don't forget the extra answer sheets and the attendance sheet.

Mr. Raj: Got it. Let's double-check everything in the morning.

8. Discussing Classroom Discipline

Ms. Kavitha: Mr. Ravi, are you facing issues with Class 7B?

Mr. Ravi: Yes, they've become a bit unruly lately.

Ms. Kavitha: Same here. I think we should have a joint session on discipline.

Mr. Ravi: That's a good idea. Maybe we can include the class teacher too.

Ms. Kavitha: Let's meet with her after school and plan it out

9. Sharing Teaching Resources

Mr. Arvind: Ms. Nandhini, do you have any activities for teaching reported speech?

Ms. Nandhini: Yes, I used a role-play activity last week. I can share the worksheet.

Mr. Arvind: That would be great! My students are struggling with the concept.

Ms. Nandhini: I'll email you the PDF. You can adapt it as needed.

Mr. Arvind: Thank you so much!

10. Welcoming a New Teacher

Ms. Leela: Hello! You must be the new history teacher.

Mr. Suman: Yes, I'm Suman. I joined today.

Ms. Leela: Welcome to the team! If you need any help, feel free to ask.

Mr. Suman: Thank you. I'm still getting familiar with the timetable.

Ms. Leela: I'll walk you through it during the break. Let's have a cup of tea.

11. Coordinating Homework Assignments

Mr. Raghav: Hi, Ms. Divya. Are you giving homework for Class 8 today?

Ms. Divya: Yes, a short grammar exercise. Why?

Mr. Raghav: I'm planning a science worksheet. I don't want to overload them.

Ms. Divya: That's thoughtful. I'll give mine as an optional activity then.

Mr. Raghav: Great! Let's inform the class teacher too.

12. Talking After Class Observation

Ms. Bhavani: Good job on your English lesson today. I observed it for the peer review.

Mr. Naresh: Thank you! I was a little nervous with observers around.

Ms. Bhavani: You handled the students well. I liked the group activity part.
Mr. Naresh: I appreciate the feedback. Any areas I can improve?
Ms. Bhavani: Maybe include a quick recap at the end. Otherwise, excellent work.

13. Discussing Student Counselling Needs

Ms. Radha: Mr. Ajay, I think we need to refer Rahul to the counsellor.
Mr. Ajay: I agree. He seems withdrawn and hasn't spoken in class lately.
Ms. Radha: I spoke to his friend who said he's facing issues at home.
Mr. Ajay: Let's talk to the counsellor and inform the principal discreetly.
Ms. Radha: Yes, the earlier we act, the better.

14. Organising a Field Trip

Ms. Shalini: Mr. Arul, would you be available to accompany us for the field trip next week?
Mr. Arul: Sure. Which class and where to?
Ms. Shalini: Class 6 to the science museum on Thursday.
Mr. Arul: Sounds good. How many students?
Ms. Shalini: Around 40. We'll need two teachers minimum.
Mr. Arul: I'll be there. Let's finalise the permission forms today.

15. Planning a Lesson Together

Mr. Manish: Ms. Iqra, we're both teaching the same class – Class 9A English.
Ms. Iqra: Yes, I was thinking we could plan the poetry unit together.
Mr. Manish: Good idea. That way we can align the content and activities.
Ms. Iqra: Let's divide the poems and share ideas for teaching methods.
Mr. Manish: Perfect. I'll make a shared folder for resources.

16. Managing a Sick Student in Class

Ms. Preethi: Mr. Keshav, one of your students, Sneha, felt dizzy during my class.
Mr. Keshav: Oh dear. Is she okay now?
Ms. Preethi: Yes, I sent her to the nurse. You may want to follow up with her.
Mr. Keshav: I'll check on her now. Thanks for informing me.

17. Conducting a Group Project

Mr. Dinesh: Ms. Asha, I'm assigning a group project to Class 10 on environmental issues.
Ms. Asha: Great! I'm teaching geography, so I'll reinforce the topic.
Mr. Dinesh: Perfect. Can we coordinate timelines to avoid overlap?
Ms. Asha: Sure. Let's plan it so they submit to both of us together.

18. Preparing for a Staff Evaluation

Ms. Reema: The school inspection is coming up next week. Are your files ready?
Mr. Arif: Almost. I need to update the lesson plans and student records.
Ms. Reema: Don't forget the co-curricular activity log.
Mr. Arif: Right! Thanks for reminding me. We should help each other review everything.

19. After a Difficult Class

Ms. Sneha: That was a tough period! Class 7C just wouldn't settle down.
Mr. Lokesh: They've been like that lately. Did you try group work?
Ms. Sneha: I did, but a few kept disturbing others.

Mr. Lokesh: I spoke to the class teacher last week. Maybe a warning note home will help.

Ms. Sneha: Yes, and I might arrange a counselling session if this continues.

20. Talking About Student Attendance

Mr. Harish: Ms. Anita, I noticed that Kiran has been absent quite often.

Ms. Anita: Yes, he's missed almost half the month.

Mr. Harish: We should inform the principal and contact his parents.

Ms. Anita: I'll speak to the office staff to get his contact details.

Mr. Harish: Let's document it too, in case we need to follow up.

21. During Exam Correction

Ms. Gayathri: Mr. Sameer, how's the correction going for Class 10 papers?

Mr. Sameer: Slow! Some answers are so hard to decipher.

Ms. Gayathri: Tell me about it! I've started keeping a checklist to speed things up.

Mr. Sameer: Good idea. I'll try that. Are we submitting marks by Friday?

Ms. Gayathri: Yes. Don't forget the internal marks too.

22. Coordinating Co-Curricular Activities

Ms. Tara: Mr. Naveen, can your students help with the stage decoration tomorrow?

Mr. Naveen: Sure. I have a few students in mind who are good at art.

Ms. Tara: Wonderful. Please send them by 10 a.m. to the auditorium.

Mr. Naveen: Done. Let me know if you need anything else.

23. Informal Chat Over Tea

Mr. Anbu: So, any weekend plans, Ms. Revathi?
Ms. Revathi: I plan to rest and read. It's been a hectic week!
Mr. Anbu: Same here. I might go for a short trip with my family.
Ms. Revathi: That sounds relaxing. Enjoy and take lots of photos!
Mr. Anbu: Will do! See you Monday!

24. Suggesting a Teaching Workshop

Ms. Farida: Mr. Hari, there's a workshop on creative writing techniques next week.
Mr. Hari: Sounds interesting! Is it online or in person?
Ms. Farida: Online, on Saturday. I've registered already.
Mr. Hari: I'll register too. Maybe we can share notes afterwards.
Ms. Farida: Sure! We can even conduct a session for our team later.

25. Talking to a New Trainee Teacher

Mr. Siva: Hi, I heard you're the new trainee in the English department.
Ms. Neelima: Yes, I joined yesterday. I'm still learning the routines.
Mr. Siva: Welcome! Don't hesitate to ask if you need anything.
Ms. Neelima: Thank you, that means a lot.
Mr. Siva: Let's catch up after your class—I can show you the resource room.

II. Parent-Teacher Conversations

1. Discussing Academic Progress

Teacher: Good morning, Mr. and Mrs. Rao. Please have a seat.
Parent: Good morning. How is our son, Arjun, performing in class?
Teacher: He is doing well in science and English, but he needs to work harder in mathematics.

Parent: We'll arrange for extra help at home.
Teacher: That will help. Also, encourage him to ask questions during class.
Parent: Absolutely. Thank you for the feedback.

2. Behavioural Issues

Teacher: Thank you for coming, Mrs. Iqbal. I wanted to speak to you about your daughter, Sara.
Parent: Is everything okay?
Teacher: She's a bright student, but lately she's been distracted and talking during lessons.
Parent: I'll talk to her. She may be going through a phase.
Teacher: Please do. I'd also suggest giving her a routine at home.
Parent: Thank you for informing me. We'll take care of it.

3. Compliments and Positive Feedback

Teacher: Mr. Sharma, I must tell you – your son Kunal is a pleasure to teach.
Parent: That's wonderful to hear. He enjoys your classes very much.
Teacher: He's always attentive, and he helps his classmates too.
Parent: Thank you. We'll continue to support him at home.
Teacher: I appreciate that. Keep up the encouragement

4. Absenteeism or Late Submission

Teacher: Mr. Thomas, I noticed that your daughter has missed several assignments.
Parent: I wasn't aware of that. She told me she was doing fine.
Teacher: She's intelligent but needs to be more consistent.
Parent: I'll ensure she completes everything. Could you send me the pending list?
Teacher: Certainly. I'll email it to you today.

III. Online Teaching Conversations

1. Starting a Virtual Class

Teacher: Good morning, everyone. Please turn on your cameras and mute your microphones.
Student: Good morning, ma'am.
Teacher: Today we are going to revise the chapter on adjectives.
Student: Ma'am, your voice is breaking.
Teacher: Okay, let me adjust my network. Please wait a moment. Can you hear me now?
Student: Yes, it's clear now

2. Dealing with a Technical Problem

Teacher: John, I can't hear you. Please check your microphone settings.
Student: One second, ma'am. I'll rejoin the meeting.
Teacher: Okay, no problem. We'll wait.
(*After rejoining*)
Student: Can you hear me now?
Teacher: Yes, now it's perfect.

3. Giving Homework in an Online Class

Teacher: I've uploaded the worksheet in the class WhatsApp group and on Google Classroom.
Student: Ma'am, what is the deadline?
Teacher: Please submit it by 5 p.m. tomorrow.
Student: Do we have to write it or type it?
Teacher: You can type it and upload a PDF. If you prefer, write it neatly and upload a clear photo.

4. Ending the Online Class

Teacher: That's all for today. Do you have any doubts?
Student: No, ma'am.
Teacher: Great. Don't forget the assignment. See you all tomorrow. Bye!
Students: Thank you, ma'am. Bye!

CHAPTER ELEVEN

COMMON PHRASES

Common Phrases for Giving Opinions (Students & Teachers)

For Students:

- I think...
- In my opinion...
- I believe that...
- From my point of view...
- To me, it seems that...
- As far as I'm concerned...
- I would say that...

For Teachers:

- I personally feel that...
- It's my view that...
- I tend to agree with...
- Let me share my opinion...
- As an educator, I believe...
- I'd suggest that...
- My experience tells me that...

Classroom Expressions for Agreeing and Disagreeing

Agreeing:

- I agree with that.
- That's a good point.
- I think so too.
- You're right about that.

Disagreeing (politely):

- I see your point, but I think...
- I'm not sure I agree.
- That's an interesting view, but...
- I respectfully disagree because...

Common Phrases for Offering – Students

Offering Help:

- Can I help you with that?
- Would you like some help?
- Do you need a hand?
- I can carry that for you.
- Shall I explain it again?
- Let me show you how to do it.

Offering Things:

- You can borrow my pen.
- Would you like my notebook?
- Here, take mine.
- I have an extra worksheet. Do you want it?

Offering to Do Something:

- I'll go get the book for you.
- I can draw the diagram on the board.
- Let me open the window.

Common Phrases for Offering – Teachers

Offering Help or Support:

- Would you like me to explain that again?
- Do you want some extra practice?
- Can I help you understand it better?
- I'm here if you need support.
- Let me know if you'd like another example.

Offering Materials or Time:

- I can give you more time to complete it.
- Would you like another worksheet?
- You may use the dictionary if needed.
- Shall I show you a video to explain it?

Offering Suggestions:

- Why don't you try reading it aloud?
- You could draw a mind map for this.
- Maybe group discussion will help you understand.
- Try writing a summary in your own words.

Common Phrases for Refusing an Invitation Politely

For Students:
1. Polite and Formal:

- Thank you for inviting me, but I won't be able to come.

- I appreciate the invitation, but I have other plans.
- I'd love to join, but I have to study for a test.
- I'm sorry, I can't make it this time.

2. Informal and Friendly:

- Sounds fun, but I've got something else going on.
- I wish I could, but I've got homework to finish.
- Thanks, but I have to be home early today.
- Maybe next time, I can't join today.

For Teachers:
1. Professional Refusals:

- Thank you for the kind invitation, but I won't be able to attend.
- I truly appreciate it, but I have a prior commitment.
- I'd love to join, but I have some responsibilities to attend to.
- It sounds wonderful, but I won't be available on that day.

2. Gentle and Encouraging:

- I wish I could be there. Please enjoy it on my behalf.
- Thank you so much. Maybe I can join next time.
- Please do send me photos—I'll definitely make it next time.

Common Phrases for Complaining Politely

For Students
1. General Classroom Issues:

- Excuse me, ma'am/sir, I'd like to say something about...
- I'm having trouble understanding this part.
- I'm sorry, but the classroom is very noisy.
- I don't think that's fair, may I explain why?
- I wasn't given a chance to speak.

2. About Other Students:

- He/She keeps disturbing me during class.
- I can't concentrate because of the noise.
- Someone is using their phone and it's distracting.

For Teachers
1. About Student Behaviour:

- I've noticed some students are not paying attention.
- There's been too much talking during lessons.
- I'm concerned about the lack of homework submissions.
- This kind of behavior is unacceptable in class.

2. To School Management (Formally):

- I'd like to bring to your attention an issue regarding...
- I have a concern about the classroom facilities.
- There has been a repeated delay in...
- It would be appreciated if the matter could be looked into.

Common Phrases for Expressing Likes

For Students:
1. Simple Expressions:

- I like reading storybooks.
- I really enjoy science experiments.
- My favourite subject is English.
- I love working in groups.
- I'm interested in maths and puzzles.
- Art is something I really like.

2. More Advanced:

- I find history fascinating.
- What I like most is solving problems.
- I'm quite fond of creative writing.
- I take great interest in current affairs.

For Teachers:
1. In Teaching Context:

- I enjoy teaching grammar with activities.
- I love when students ask thoughtful questions.
- I like using visuals and real-life examples.
- I prefer interactive sessions over lectures.
- Group work is something I always encourage.

2. When Giving Feedback:

- I liked how you explained that.
- I really enjoyed your presentation.
- I appreciate the effort you've put in.
- I was impressed by your creativity.

Common Phrases for Asking Opinions

For Students:
1. To classmates:

- What do you think about this topic?
- Do you agree with my answer?
- What's your opinion on this?
- How do you feel about the story?
- Do you think this solution is correct?
- Would you choose the same answer? Why or why not?

2. To the teacher:

- Do you think this method is okay?
- What's your view on my answer?
- Should I improve this part?
- Do you agree with what I said?

For Teachers:
1. To students:

- What do you think about this idea?
- How do you feel about the character's actions?
- Do you agree or disagree? Why?
- What's your point of view?
- Would anyone like to share a different opinion?
- What's your take on this situation?

2. To colleagues or during discussions:

- What's your perspective on this teaching method?
- How do you feel about using digital tools in class?
- Would you recommend this book for our students?
- Do you think this strategy will work?

Common Phrases for Expressing Dislikes

For Students
1. General Expressions:

- I don't like this topic very much.
- I'm not really interested in this chapter.
- I find this subject a bit boring.
- This activity is difficult for me.
- I'm not comfortable doing group work.
- I prefer writing to speaking.

2. Polite and Constructive:

- This method doesn't work well for me.
- I find it hard to focus during long lectures.
- I struggle with this kind of question.
- I don't enjoy this, but I'll try to do it.

For Teachers
1. Professional and Diplomatic:

- I'm not a fan of this textbook layout.
- I don't find this technique very effective.
- I prefer not to rely on rote learning.
- This approach doesn't always engage the students.
- I'd rather use interactive methods.

2. In Feedback Context:

- I noticed some students didn't enjoy the activity.
- This type of question seems to confuse many students.
- The class doesn't respond well to this format.

Common Phrases for Expressing Gratitude

For Students
1. To Teachers or Classmates:

- Thank you, ma'am/sir.
- Thanks a lot for helping me.
- I really appreciate your explanation.
- Thank you for your support.
- I'm grateful for your guidance.
- Thanks for lending me your notes.
- That was very kind of you.

2. In Formal Situations:

- I sincerely thank you for the opportunity.
- It means a lot to me.
- I'm truly thankful for your feedback.

For Teachers
1. To Students or Colleagues:

- Thank you for your attention.
- I appreciate your effort in today's class.
- Thanks for participating actively.
- I'm grateful for your cooperation.
- Thank you for completing the work on time.
- Thanks for your help in organising the event.

2. In Staff Meetings or Official Notes:

- I'd like to express my gratitude to the team.
- I truly value your contributions.
- Thanks for your support throughout the project.

Common Phrases for Apologizing

For Students
1. Simple and Polite Apologies:

- I'm sorry, ma'am/sir.
- I apologize for being late.
- Sorry, I forgot my homework.
- Please excuse me for the mistake.
- I didn't mean to interrupt.
- Sorry, I wasn't paying attention.

2. More Formal or Reflective:

- I sincerely apologize for the confusion.

- It won't happen again.
- I'll make sure to correct it next time.
- I'm really sorry for the inconvenience.

For Teachers
1. To Students:

- I'm sorry for the delay in giving feedback.
- I apologize for the confusion caused earlier.
- Please excuse the interruption.
- I should have explained that better. Thank you for your patience.

2. To Colleagues or Management:

- I apologize for the oversight.
- Sorry, I missed your message.
- I regret the misunderstanding.
- Please accept my apologies for the delay.

Common Phrases for Expressing Sympathy

For Students
1. To Classmates:

- I'm sorry to hear that.
- That must be really hard.
- I hope you feel better soon.
- Don't worry, things will get better.
- Take care. Let me know if I can help.
- That's really unfortunate. I'm here if you need anything.

For Teachers
1. To Students:

- I'm sorry you're going through this.
- Take your time. We're here for you.
- It's okay to feel upset.
- If you need to talk, I'm available.
- I understand this is difficult.
- Please let me know how I can support you.

2. To Colleagues:

- I'm sorry to hear about your loss.
- Thinking of you during this difficult time.
- Please accept my deepest sympathies.
- If there's anything I can do, let me know.
- Wishing you strength and peace.

CHAPTER TWELVE

PAIRS OF OFTEN CONFUSED ENGLISH WORDS

1. Accept vs Except

- **Accept:** To receive or agree to something
  She accepted the award with gratitude.
- **Except:** To exclude or leave out
  Everyone was invited except James.

2. Affect vs Effect

- **Affect:** A verb meaning to influence
  The cold weather affected my mood.
- **Effect:** A noun meaning the result
  The new policy had a positive effect on productivity.

3. Compliment vs Complement

- **Compliment:** A polite expression of praise
  He gave her a compliment on her dress.
- **Complement:** Something that completes or matches well
  The red wine complements the steak perfectly.

4. Principal vs Principle

- **Principal**: A person in charge or main/most important
  The school principal greeted the students.
- **Principle**: A fundamental belief or rule
  She always acts according to her principles.

5. Stationary vs Stationery

- **Stationary**: Not moving or still
  The car remained stationary at the traffic light.
- **Stationery**: Paper, pens, and writing supplies
  I bought new stationery for school.

6. Advice vs Advise

- **Advice**: A noun meaning a suggestion or recommendation
  My teacher gave me good advice about studying.
- **Advise**: A verb meaning to suggest or recommend
  I advise you to take regular breaks while studying.

7. Lose vs Loose

- **Lose**: To misplace or not win
  Don't lose your keys again!
- **Loose**: Not tight or free
  These shoes are too loose on my feet.

8. Farther vs Further

- **Farther**: Physical distance
  The park is farther than the library.

- **Further**: More in depth or abstract distance
  We need to discuss this issue further.

9. Than vs Then

- **Than**: Used in comparisons
  She is taller than her brother.
- **Then**: Refers to time or result
  We went shopping, then we had lunch.

10. Desert vs Dessert

- **Desert**: A dry, arid land
  Camels live in the desert.
- **Dessert**: Sweet food eaten after a meal
  We had ice cream for dessert.

11. Capital vs Capitol

- **Capital**: A city or money
  Tokyo is the capital of Japan.
- **Capitol**: A government building
  The lawmakers met inside the capitol.

12. Ensure vs Insure

- **Ensure**: To make sure
  Please ensure all doors are locked before you leave.
- **Insure**: To protect financially with insurance
  We insured our house against damage.

13. Historic vs Historical

- **Historic**: Famous or important in history
  It was a historic day for the nation.
- **Historical**: Relating to history in general
  She loves reading historical novels.

14. Emigrate vs Immigrate

- **Emigrate**: To leave one's country
  They emigrated from India in the 1980s.
- **Immigrate**: To move to a new country
  She immigrated to Canada for work.

15. Allusion vs Illusion

- **Allusion**: An indirect reference
  The poem contains an allusion to Greek mythology.
- **Illusion**: A false or misleading appearance
  The magician created the illusion of flying.

16. Precede vs Proceed

- **Precede**: To come before
  A brief speech will precede the award ceremony.
- **Proceed**: To go ahead or continue
  Please proceed with your presentation.

17. Acceptable vs Accessible

- **Acceptable**: Good enough or satisfactory
  Your behavior is not acceptable here.
- **Accessible**: Easy to reach or use
  The museum is accessible to people with disabilities.

18. Complementary vs Complimentary

- **Complementary**: Matching or completing
  Their skills are complementary in the project.
- **Complimentary**: Free or flattering
  The hotel offered complimentary breakfast.

19. Altogether vs All together

- **Altogether**: Completely or entirely
  I am altogether confused by this explanation.
- **All together**: All in one place or group
  We sat all together at the front.

20. Assure vs Ensure vs Insure

- **Assure**: To promise or comfort someone
  I assure you that everything will be okay.
- **Ensure**: To make certain
  Ensure that all documents are signed.
- **Insure**: To cover against loss or damage
  They insured the building for $1 million.

21. Borrow vs Lend

- **Borrow**: To take something temporarily
  Can I borrow your pen?
- **Lend**: To give something temporarily
  I will lend you my book tomorrow.

22. Cite vs Site vs Sight

- **Cite**: To quote or refer to
  You must cite your sources in the report.

- **Site**: A location or place
  This is the site of the new library.
- **Sight**: The ability to see or something seen
  The mountain view was a beautiful sight.

23. Elicit vs Illicit

- **Elicit**: To draw out (a response)
  The question elicited a strong reaction.
- **Illicit**: Illegal or forbidden
  He was caught with illicit drugs.

24. Imply vs Infer

- **Imply**: To suggest indirectly
  He didn't say it directly, but he implied it.
- **Infer**: To understand or conclude from clues
  We inferred that she was upset from her tone.

25. Disinterested vs Uninterested

- **Disinterested**: Unbiased or impartial
  A judge must remain disinterested in the case.
- **Uninterested**: Not interested or bored
  She looked uninterested in the conversation.

26. Explicit vs Implicit

- **Explicit**: Clearly stated, leaving no room for doubt
  The instructions were explicit and easy to follow.
- **Implicit**: Implied or understood without being directly stated
  There was an implicit threat in his tone.

27. Later vs Latter

- **Later:** Refers to time in the future
  We'll finish the project later today.
- **Latter:** Refers to the second of two mentioned items
  Of tea and coffee, I prefer the latter.

28. Moral vs Morale

- **Moral:** A lesson or principle of right and wrong
  The story had a clear moral.
- **Morale:** The mood or spirit of a group
  The team's morale was high after the win.

29. Prescribe vs Proscribe

- **Prescribe:** To recommend or authorize (often medicine)
  The doctor prescribed antibiotics.
- **Proscribe:** To forbid, especially by law
  The government proscribed the use of certain chemicals.

30. Proceed vs Precede

- **Proceed:** To go forward
  Please proceed with your explanation.
- **Precede:** To come before
  The appetizer preceded the main course.

31. Respectfully vs Respectively

- **Respectfully:** In a polite or courteous way
  He respectfully disagreed with his teacher.
- **Respectively:** In the order previously mentioned
  John and Mike scored 85 and 90, respectively.

32. Dual vs Duel

- **Dual**: Having two parts
  She has dual citizenship.
- **Duel**: A formal fight between two people
  The movie featured an intense sword duel.

33. Discreet vs Discrete

- **Discreet**: Careful, tactful
  She was discreet in handling the sensitive issue.
- **Discrete**: Separate or distinct
  The course is divided into five discrete modules.

34. Foreword vs Forward

- **Foreword**: An introductory section in a book
  The author wrote a touching foreword.
- **Forward**: Toward the front
  He stepped forward to receive his award.

35. Eminent vs Imminent

- **Eminent**: Famous or respected
  She is an eminent scientist.
- **Imminent**: About to happen
  A storm is imminent.

36. Loose vs Lose

- **Loose**: Not tight
  This shirt is too loose on me.
- **Lose**: To misplace or not win
  Don't lose your phone again!

37. Personal vs Personnel

- **Personal**: Relating to a person
  She kept a personal diary.
- **Personnel**: Staff or employees
  The HR department manages all personnel issues.

38. Presume vs Assume

- **Presume**: To suppose based on probability
  I presume he's already left the office.
- **Assume**: To take for granted without proof
  Don't assume she's not coming.

39. Reign vs Rein

- **Reign**: Rule or authority (usually of royalty)
  The king's reign lasted 40 years.
- **Rein**: A strap or control mechanism
  He pulled the reins to stop the horse.

40. Than vs That

- **Than**: Used for comparisons
  She is faster than I am.
- **That**: Used to identify or specify
  This is the book that I was looking for.

41. Wave vs Waive

- **Wave**: Move back and forth or gesture
  She waved goodbye to her friend.

- **Waive:** To give up a right or claim voluntarily
  The bank waived the late fee.

42. Sight vs Site

- **Sight:** Ability to see or something seen
  The mountains were a beautiful sight.
- **Site:** Location or place
  This is the site of the future mall.

43. Adapt vs Adopt

- **Adapt:** To adjust to new conditions
  He adapted quickly to the new environment.
- **Adopt:** To take as one's own
  They adopted a baby from Korea.

44. Altogether vs All together

- **Altogether:** Entirely or completely
  The experience was altogether enjoyable.
- **All together:** Everyone in one group or place
  We travelled all together by bus.

45. Among vs Between

- **Among:** Used when referring to more than two
  She divided the chocolates among her five friends.
- **Between:** Used when referring to two
  The ball rolled between the two chairs.

46. Council vs Counsel

- **Council**: A group that makes decisions
  The student council organized the event.
- **Counsel**: Advice or a lawyer
  She sought legal counsel.

47. Desperate vs Disparate

- **Desperate**: Feeling hopeless or urgent
  He was desperate to find a job.
- **Disparate**: Essentially different
  They had disparate views on politics.

48. Historic vs Historical

- **Historic**: Very important in history
  They visited a historic battlefield.
- **Historical**: Relating to past events
  She enjoys reading historical novels.

49. Ingenious vs Ingenuous

- **Ingenious**: Clever or inventive
  She came up with an ingenious solution.
- **Ingenuous**: Honest and innocent
  He gave an ingenuous smile.

50. Prescribe vs Describe

- **Prescribe**: To recommend or authorize (typically medicine)
  The doctor prescribed some antibiotics.
- **Describe**: To give details about something
  Can you describe the person you saw?

51. All ready vs Already

- **All ready**: Completely prepared
  We are all ready to start the event.
- **Already**: By this time, earlier than expected
  She has already finished her homework.

52. Bear vs Bare

- **Bear**: To carry, endure, or the animal
  I can't bear the pain anymore.
- **Bare**: Uncovered or exposed
  He walked barefoot on the bare ground.

53. Brake vs Break

- **Brake**: A device for slowing a vehicle
  He hit the brake suddenly.
- **Break**: To shatter or a pause
  Take a break after finishing the work.

54. Canvas vs Canvass

- **Canvas**: A type of strong fabric
  The artist painted on a canvas.
- **Canvass**: To solicit votes or opinions
  They canvassed the neighborhood for support.

55. Censor vs Censure

- **Censor**: To suppress content
  The film was censored for violence.
- **Censure**: To criticize strongly
  The official was censured for misconduct.

56. Climactic vs Climatic

- **Climactic**: Relating to a climax
  The movie ended with a climactic scene.
- **Climatic**: Related to climate
  Climatic changes affect agriculture.

57. Confidant vs Confident

- **Confidant**: A trusted person
  She is my closest confidant.
- **Confident**: Self-assured
  He felt confident before the exam.

58. Conscience vs Conscious

- **Conscience**: Inner sense of right and wrong
  His conscience bothered him after the lie.
- **Conscious**: Awake or aware
  She was conscious during the operation.

59. Disassemble vs Dissemble

- **Disassemble**: To take apart
  They disassembled the machine for repair.
- **Dissemble**: To disguise true feelings
  He tried to dissemble his disappointment.

60. Dual vs Duel

- **Dual**: Two parts or functions
  She holds dual citizenship.

- **Duel**: A formal fight
  The knights fought a duel.

61. Defuse vs Diffuse

- **Defuse**: To reduce tension or danger
  They tried to defuse the argument.
- **Diffuse**: To spread widely
  The perfume diffused through the room.

62. Flaunt vs Flout

- **Flaunt**: To show off
  He flaunted his new car.
- **Flout**: To disregard or disobey
  They flouted the rules openly.

63. Grisly vs Grizzly

- **Grisly**: Horrible, gruesome
  It was a grisly crime scene.
- **Grizzly**: A type of bear
  We saw a grizzly bear in the forest.

64. Hoard vs Horde

- **Hoard**: A stash or store
  He hoarded food during the pandemic.
- **Horde**: A large group
  A horde of fans gathered at the stadium.

65. Illegible vs Illegal

- **Illegible**: Not readable
  Your handwriting is almost illegible.
- **Illegal**: Against the law
  Selling endangered species is illegal.

66. Imply vs Implicate

- **Imply**: To suggest indirectly
  She implied that I was wrong.
- **Implicate**: To show involvement
  He was implicated in the scandal.

67. Judicial vs Judicious

- **Judicial**: Related to the law or courts
  The judicial system must be fair.
- **Judicious**: Wise or sensible
  She made a judicious decision.

68. Lightning vs Lightening

- **Lightning**: Electrical discharge
  The lightning struck the tree.
- **Lightening**: Making something lighter
  She's lightening her hair color.

69. Militate vs Mitigate

- **Militate**: To work against
  His poor attitude will militate against success.
- **Mitigate**: To reduce severity
  The doctor gave medicine to mitigate the pain.

70. Ordinance vs Ordnance

- **Ordinance:** A law or regulation
  The city passed a noise ordinance.
- **Ordnance:** Military weapons
  The army stored ordnance in the bunker.

71. Persecute vs Prosecute

- **Persecute:** To harass or oppress
  They were persecuted for their beliefs.
- **Prosecute:** To bring legal action against
  The government decided to prosecute the criminal.

72. Prescribe vs Proscribe

- **Prescribe:** To recommend (especially medicine)
  The doctor prescribed antibiotics.
- **Proscribe:** To forbid
  The law proscribes discrimination.

73. Raise vs Raze

- **Raise:** To lift or increase
  They raised their hands to answer.
- **Raze:** To completely destroy
  The building was razed to make space.

74. Respectable vs Respective

- **Respectable:** Worthy of respect
  He comes from a respectable family.
- **Respective:** Relating to each one individually
  They returned to their respective homes.

75. Sensual vs Sensuous

- **Sensual**: Relating to physical pleasures
  He was drawn to her sensual charm.
- **Sensuous**: Appealing to the senses
  The painting has a sensuous beauty.

76. Than vs Then

- **Than**: Used in comparisons
  He is taller than his brother.
- **Then**: Refers to time or consequence
  We ate lunch, then went out.

77. Their vs There vs They're

- **Their**: Possessive
  Their car is parked outside.
- **There**: Refers to a place
  Put the book over there.
- **They're**: Contraction of "they are"
  They're going to the museum.

78. To vs Too vs Two

- **To**: Preposition
  I'm going to school.
- **Too**: Also or excessively
  I want to come too.
- **Two**: Number
  I have two sisters.

79. Vain vs Vein vs Vane

- **Vain**: Proud or fruitless
  She is too vain about her looks.
- **Vein**: Blood vessel
  The nurse found a vein easily.
- **Vane**: A blade or weather instrument
  The weather vane turned with the wind.

80. Whose vs Who's

- **Whose**: Possessive
  Whose book is this?
- **Who's**: Contraction of "who is"
  Who's coming to the party?

81. Adapt vs Adept

- **Adapt**: To adjust to new conditions
  He had to adapt quickly to the new environment.
- **Adept**: Skilled or proficient
  She is adept at solving complex math problems.

82. Adverse vs Averse

- **Adverse**: Unfavorable or harmful
  The medication may cause adverse side effects.
- **Averse**: Having a strong dislike
  She is averse to taking unnecessary risks.

83. Amoral vs Immoral

- **Amoral**: Lacking a sense of right and wrong
  The machine is amoral—it has no ethics.
- **Immoral**: Deliberately wrong or unethical
  Cheating is considered immoral behavior.

84. Appraise vs Apprise

- **Appraise**: To evaluate or assess
  The jeweler appraised the diamond at $5000.
- **Apprise**: To inform or notify
  Please apprise me of any changes in the schedule.

85. Assent vs Ascent

- **Assent**: Agreement or approval
  The manager gave his assent to the proposal.
- **Ascent**: An upward movement
  The hikers began their ascent up the mountain.

86. Blond vs Blonde

- **Blond**: (Typically used for males) fair-haired
  The blond boy waved at us.
- **Blonde**: (Typically used for females) fair-haired
  She is a blonde actress from Sweden.

87. Childish vs Childlike

- **Childish**: Immature
  Stop being so childish during the meeting.
- **Childlike**: Innocent or pure
  She had a childlike sense of wonder.

88. Dependant vs Dependent

- **Dependant**: A person who relies on someone else (British spelling)
  He has two dependants listed on his insurance.

- **Dependent**: Relying on something or someone
  The result is dependent on the weather.

89. Discrete vs Discreet

- **Discrete**: Separate, distinct
  The report is divided into discrete sections.
- **Discreet**: Tactful, not drawing attention
  Please be discreet about the surprise party.

90. Elicit vs Illicit

- **Elicit**: To draw out
  The teacher tried to elicit answers from the class.
- **Illicit**: Forbidden by law
  They were caught with illicit substances.

91. Ensure vs Assure

- **Ensure**: To make sure
  Ensure the lights are off before leaving.
- **Assure**: To comfort or promise
  I assure you, everything will be fine.

92. Famous vs Notorious

- **Famous**: Well-known for good reasons
  She is a famous author.
- **Notorious**: Well-known for bad reasons
  He is notorious for skipping school.

93. Gorilla vs Guerrilla

- **Gorilla:** A large ape
  We saw a gorilla at the zoo.
- **Guerrilla:** A member of a small fighting force
  The guerrilla fighters launched a surprise attack.

94. Human vs Humane

- **Human:** A person
  Humans need water and food to survive.
- **Humane:** Showing kindness or compassion
  She supports humane treatment of animals.

95. Loose vs Lose

- **Loose:** Not tight
  My belt is too loose.
- **Lose:** To misplace or be defeated
  Don't lose your phone again.

96. Maybe vs May be

- **Maybe:** Perhaps (adverb)
  Maybe we'll go out tonight.
- **May be:** Might be (verb phrase)
  She may be late to class.

97. Precede vs Proceed

- **Precede:** To come before
  The introduction precedes the main topic.
- **Proceed:** To go ahead
  Please proceed with your presentation.

98. Quiet vs Quite

- **Quiet:** Silent or calm
  Please be quiet in the library.
- **Quite:** Very or completely
  This movie is quite interesting.

99. Reluctant vs Reticent

- **Reluctant:** Unwilling or hesitant
  He was reluctant to answer the question.
- **Reticent:** Reserved, not speaking much
  She is reticent about her personal life.

100. Verbal vs Oral

- **Verbal:** Related to words (spoken or written)
  The contract must be in verbal or written form.
- **Oral:** Specifically spoken
  The student gave an oral presentation.

CHAPTER THIRTEEN

COMMONLY MISUSED WORDS OR EXPRESSIONS IN ENGLISH

Commonly Misused Words or Expressions in English along with their Correct and Incorrect Usage and Explanations:

1. Literally

Incorrect: *I literally died laughing.*

Correct: : *I figuratively died laughing.*

2. Unique

Incorrect: *That is very unique.*

Correct: *That is unique.*

"Unique" means one of a kind — it cannot be modified by "very" or "more."

3. Irregardless

Incorrect: *Irregardless of the outcome, I'm happy.*

Correct: *Regardless of the outcome, I'm happy.*

"Irregardless" is nonstandard and should be avoided.

4. Presently

Incorrect: *I'm presently eating dinner.*

Correct: *'ll arrive presently.*

"Presently" traditionally means "soon," not "right now."

5. Disinterested

Incorrect: *She was disinterested in the game.*

Correct: *She was uninterested in the game.*

"Disinterested" means impartial, not lacking interest.

6. Redundant

Incorrect: *Let's repeat this again for redundancy.*

Correct: *Let's repeat this again.*

"Redundant" already means unnecessarily repetitive.

7. Bemused

Incorrect: *He was bemused by the joke.*

Correct: *He was bemused (confused), not amused.*

"Bemused" means puzzled, not entertained.

8. Ironic

Incorrect: *It's ironic that I forgot my umbrella when it rained.*

Correct: *It's unfortunate, not ironic.*

"Ironic" means the opposite of what you expect, not just bad luck.

9. Plethora

Incorrect: *There was a plethora of problems.*

Correct: *There was a plethora of options.*

"Plethora" refers to an excess or abundance, often positive.

10. Peruse

Incorrect: *I just perused the article quickly.*

Correct: *I perused the article carefully.*

"Peruse" means to read thoroughly, not skim.

11. Chronic

Incorrect: *She had a chronic headache yesterday.*

Correct: *She has a chronic headache condition.*

"Chronic" means long-term, not one-time.

12. Enormity

Incorrect: *The enormity of the building amazed us.*

Correct: *The enormity of the crime shocked us.*

"Enormity" means great wickedness, not great size.

13. Conversate

Incorrect: *We conversated for hours.*

Correct: *We conversed for hours.*

"Conversate" is a nonstandard form of "converse."

14. Anxious

Incorrect: *I'm anxious to meet her.*

Correct: *I'm eager to meet her.*

"Anxious" implies worry, while "eager" implies excitement.

15. Fulsome

Incorrect: *She gave a fulsome compliment.*

Correct: *She gave a sincere compliment.*

"Fulsome" means excessively flattering, sometimes insincere.

16. Nonplussed

Incorrect: *She was nonplussed and kept going.*

Correct: *She was nonplussed and confused.*

"Nonplussed" means bewildered, not unaffected.

17. Discreet

Incorrect: *She wore a discreet dress (meant distinct).*

Correct: *She was discreet about the news.*

"Discreet" means tactful; "discrete" means separate.

18. Appraise vs Apprise

Incorrect: *He apprised the value of the car.*

Correct: *He appraised the value of the car.*

"Appraise" means to evaluate; "Apprise" means to inform.

19. Infer vs Imply

Incorrect: *He implied that I was wrong (meant inferred).*

Correct: *He implied I was wrong; I inferred it from his tone.*

"Imply" is done by the speaker; "infer" is done by the listener.

20. Momentarily

Incorrect: *I will stay here momentarily.*

Correct: *I will arrive momentarily.*

In US English, "momentarily" often means "soon," not "for a short time."

21. Aggravate

Incorrect: His lies aggravated me. *(meant annoyed)*

Correct: Smoking can aggravate asthma symptoms.

22. Discreet vs Discrete

Incorrect: She made a discrete suggestion. *(meant tactful)*

Correct: She made a discreet suggestion about improving the lesson.

23. Nauseous

Incorrect: I feel nauseous. *(meant nauseated)*

Correct: The nauseous smell made him feel sick.

24. Panacea

Incorrect: Yoga is a panacea for all problems. *(overused)*

Correct: There is no panacea for poverty.

25. Ambiguous vs Ambivalent

Incorrect: He gave an ambivalent answer. *(meant ambiguous)*

Correct: Her statement was ambiguous, leaving us unsure of her stance.

26. Decimate

Incorrect: The city was decimated. *(meant destroyed completely)*

Correct: The disease decimated the population, killing one in ten.

27. Ultimate

Incorrect: That's the ultimate phone! *(meant best)*

Correct: The ultimate goal of education is wisdom.

28. Travesty

Incorrect: That test was a travesty. *(meant difficult)*

Correct: The unfair trial was a travesty of justice.

29. Literally

Incorrect: He was literally glowing with pride.

Correct: The house literally shook during the earthquake.

30. Overwhelm vs Underwhelm

Incorrect: I was very underwhelmed. *(used humorously)*

Correct: The dull speech underwhelmed the audience.

31. Historic

Incorrect: We visited a historic pizza place. *(meant old)*

Correct: The signing of the treaty was a historic moment.

32. Luxuriant vs Luxurious

Incorrect: She wore a luxuriant dress. *(meant luxurious)*

Correct: The rainforest had luxuriant vegetation.

33. Disinterested

Incorrect: He's disinterested in chess.

Correct: A disinterested judge is essential for a fair trial.

34. Momentarily

Incorrect: He stayed momentarily. *(meant briefly)*

Correct: The train will arrive momentarily.

35. Noisome

Incorrect: The kids were noisome. *(meant noisy)*

Correct: The garbage emitted a noisome stench.

36. Enervate

Incorrect: The drink enervated me. *(meant energized)*

Correct: The heat enervated the runners.

37. Inflammable

Incorrect: It's safe—it's inflammable.

Correct: Keep away from open flame, this material is highly inflammable.

38. Historic vs Historical

Incorrect: It's a historical moment!

Correct: The Berlin Wall falling was a historic event.

39. Definite vs Definitive

Incorrect: That was the definite guide. *(meant final)*

Correct: This is the definitive biography of the poet.

40. Sensual vs Sensuous

Incorrect: The painting is sensual. *(meant sensuous)*

Correct: The sculpture has a sensuous beauty.

CHAPTER FOURTEEN

CONVERSATION BETWEEN TEACHER AND PARENT

1. General Academic Progress

Parent: Good morning, ma'am. How is my child doing in class?
Teacher: Good morning! Your child is doing well overall. He's attentive and completes his assignments on time.
Parent: That's good to know. How is he performing in tests?
Teacher: He scores well in English and Science, but his Math grades could be a bit higher.
Parent: Oh, I see. Is it a conceptual issue or a problem with practice?
Teacher: Mostly a need for regular practice. He understands concepts but needs to apply them more consistently.
Parent: We'll make sure he practices daily. Anything else we should focus on?
Teacher: He could improve his handwriting. Neater work will help with presentation and marks.
Parent: Thank you. I'll encourage him to take that seriously.
Teacher: Also, he's very polite and respectful in class. We appreciate his behavior.
Parent: Thank you so much for your support and feedback.

2. Behavior and Discipline

Teacher: Thank you for coming today. I'd like to talk about your child's classroom behavior.
Parent: Is something wrong?
Teacher: Not major, but he tends to talk to his friends during lessons, which can be distracting.
Parent: I see. He can be quite talkative at home too.
Teacher: He's friendly and enthusiastic, but he needs to learn when it's appropriate to speak.
Parent: I completely understand. We'll talk to him about classroom discipline.
Teacher: Thank you. Also, we've noticed he's quite creative, especially during group activities.
Parent: That's nice to hear. He enjoys drawing and storytelling.
Teacher: That's evident. We encourage such talents but with balanced discipline.
Parent: Yes, balance is important. Please feel free to update us if the issue continues.
Teacher: Absolutely. Thank you for your cooperation.

3. Poor Academic Performance

Parent: I'm concerned about my daughter's marks, especially in Math and Science.
Teacher: Yes, I've noticed she struggles with those subjects.
Parent: What do you think the issue is? Lack of understanding or confidence?
Teacher: A bit of both. She hesitates to ask questions even when she doesn't understand.
Parent: That sounds like her. She's a little shy.
Teacher: I'll try to engage her more in class and encourage her to speak up.
Parent: Thank you. We'll also try to boost her confidence at home.
Teacher: It might help to revise key concepts daily and practice sample problems.
Parent: We'll set up a schedule for that. Would tuition be helpful?
Teacher: Yes, a little extra support might benefit her for now.

Parent: Thank you for your honest feedback. We'll work on it.

4. Praising a Student

Teacher: I wanted to take a moment to praise your son. He's doing exceptionally well.
Parent: Really? That's wonderful to hear.
Teacher: Yes, he's very dedicated and often helps others during group work.
Parent: We always encourage him to be cooperative and kind.
Teacher: It definitely shows. He's also very responsible with his homework.
Parent: That's great. Does he participate in class activities?
Teacher: Very much. He volunteers for reading and group discussions.
Parent: We're glad he's enjoying school.
Teacher: He has strong leadership qualities as well.
Parent: Thank you for nurturing those skills. We appreciate your support.
Teacher: It's a pleasure teaching him. Keep encouraging him at home.

5. Attendance Issues

Teacher: I noticed your daughter has missed quite a few classes this term.
Parent: Yes, she's been unwell with a seasonal illness.
Teacher: I hope she's feeling better now.
Parent: Much better, thank you. We've been cautious with her recovery.
Teacher: That's understandable, but she has fallen behind a bit in coursework.
Parent: Oh, that's concerning. Can we get the missed assignments?
Teacher: Of course. I'll prepare a list and share the worksheets.
Parent: We'll help her catch up over the weekend.
Teacher: Also, let her feel free to ask questions in class.
Parent: Certainly. Thank you for understanding and your guidance.

6. Requesting Support at Home

Teacher: I'd like to speak with you briefly about your child's homework routine.

Parent: Yes, please go ahead.

Teacher: He completes tasks, but they are often rushed and lack detail.

Parent: Hmm, I've noticed he doesn't spend much time on it at home either.

Teacher: If he spends even 30 minutes focused, it will make a big difference.

Parent: I'll create a study schedule and supervise it.

Teacher: That would be very helpful. He's capable and just needs consistency.

Parent: Does he participate in class?

Teacher: Yes, but he sometimes lacks confidence. More practice at home can build that.

Parent: We'll support him. Thank you for pointing it out.

Teacher: Thank you for your cooperation.

7. Parent Raising Concerns

Parent: My son mentioned he's being teased by a group of students during break time.

Teacher: I'm very sorry to hear that. Has he shared any specific details?

Parent: He said they make fun of his stammering sometimes.

Teacher: That's unacceptable. I'll speak to him and the other students immediately.

Parent: Thank you. He's been hesitant to come to school because of it.

Teacher: We take such concerns seriously and ensure a safe environment.

Parent: We really appreciate that.

Teacher: I'll also brief our class teacher and the counselor for further support.

Parent: That's a good idea. Please let us know how we can help.

Teacher: Just keep encouraging him to speak confidently.

Parent: Absolutely. Thank you for your quick response.

8. Parent Concerned About Child's Shyness

Parent: Hello ma'am, I'm a bit worried. My daughter is very quiet in class.

Teacher: Yes, she is reserved, but she's also very observant and polite.

Parent: She's always been shy. I'm worried she might miss out on opportunities.

Teacher: I understand. We're working on gently encouraging her to speak up in group tasks.

Parent: Does she participate in any classroom activities?

Teacher: She does when prompted. She shines in art and writing assignments.

Parent: That's good to hear. Should we try anything at home?

Teacher: Yes, maybe roleplay short presentations or reading aloud to build confidence.

Parent: That's a great idea. I'll start with bedtime storytelling sessions.

Teacher: Wonderful. Small steps will help her open up gradually.

9. Teacher Addressing Late Submissions

Teacher: Thank you for coming. I'd like to talk about your son's late homework.

Parent: Oh, really? He says he completes everything.

Teacher: He does, but often submits work a day or two after the deadline.

Parent: I wasn't aware of that. I'll make sure we check his planner daily.

Teacher: That will help. He's smart and understands the work.

Parent: Is he missing out on marks due to late submissions?

Teacher: Sometimes, yes. Timeliness is important for overall assessment.

Parent: We'll definitely focus on improving this habit.

Teacher: Thank you. His class participation is good, so with regular submissions, he'll do very well.

Parent: I appreciate the update. Please inform us if it happens again.

10. Teacher Recommending Extracurricular Involvement

Teacher: Your child is academically sound, but I'd recommend more extracurricular activities.

Parent: Really? We thought it might distract from studies.

Teacher: Not at all. Activities like sports, drama, or debate can boost confidence and social skills.

Parent: That makes sense. She enjoys drawing and music.

Teacher: That's great! Our school art club would be a perfect fit.
Parent: Can we enroll her mid-term?
Teacher: Yes, just fill out the form at the front office.
Parent: Wonderful. Do these activities impact her grades?
Teacher: Not negatively. In fact, they help with focus and time management.
Parent: Thank you. We'll encourage her to join.
Teacher: She'll enjoy it, and it will help her grow holistically.

11. Transitioning to a New Grade

Parent: We're a little nervous about our child moving to high school next year.
Teacher: That's understandable. It's a big transition, but she's ready.
Parent: Do you think she'll cope well with the academic load?
Teacher: She's organized and disciplined. Those are key strengths for high school.
Parent: Should we begin preparing her at home?
Teacher: Yes, especially in time management and basic research skills.
Parent: What about emotional adjustment?
Teacher: We'll support her through counseling sessions and peer mentoring programs.
Parent: That's reassuring.
Teacher: With continued support from both school and home, she'll do well.
Parent: Thank you for your encouragement.

12. Parent Appreciating the Teacher

Parent: I just wanted to thank you for the difference you've made in my son's life.
Teacher: That's very kind of you to say. He's a pleasure to teach.
Parent: We've seen a big change in his attitude toward learning this year.
Teacher: I've seen him become more confident and curious.
Parent: You've really helped bring out his strengths.
Teacher: It's a team effort. You've clearly supported him well at home.

Parent: We just followed your suggestions after the last meeting.
Teacher: He's also very kind to his peers, which is commendable.
Parent: That means a lot to us. Thank you again.
Teacher: It's my privilege to guide students like him.

13. Parent Asking About Exam Preparation

Parent: Exams are coming up. How can we help our daughter prepare effectively?
Teacher: Start with a study timetable covering all subjects.
Parent: She struggles most with Science.
Teacher: Then allocate extra time for Science, and revise with diagrams and flashcards.
Parent: Should she practice old question papers?
Teacher: Absolutely. It builds confidence and time management.
Parent: What's the best way to review long answers?
Teacher: Encourage summarizing and using keywords instead of rote memorization.
Parent: Should she stay up late before exams?
Teacher: No, enough sleep is crucial. Light revision in the evening is best.
Parent: Thank you. This is very helpful.
Teacher: I'm always here to help. Let her reach out if she has doubts.

14. Discussing Health or Special Needs

Parent: My son was recently diagnosed with mild dyslexia. How can the school support him?
Teacher: Thank you for informing us. We'll make necessary adjustments.
Parent: Will he get extra time for assignments?
Teacher: Yes. We'll also avoid marking minor spelling errors in certain tasks.
Parent: That's thoughtful. He feels anxious during reading aloud.
Teacher: We'll let him opt out of that for now and focus on confidence-building.
Parent: Should we inform all teachers?
Teacher: I'll coordinate with the subject teachers and counselor.

Parent: What about peer teasing?

Teacher: We'll handle it firmly. His safety and dignity come first.

Parent: Thank you. We're relieved to have your support.

Teacher: We're committed to inclusive learning.

15. Addressing Overuse of Mobile Phones

Teacher: I've noticed your child seems distracted in class lately.

Parent: Really? He doesn't mention anything at home.

Teacher: It could be due to excessive mobile usage. He often seems tired and inattentive.

Parent: That might be true. He spends a lot of time on his phone at night.

Teacher: It's affecting his focus and participation.

Parent: We'll start limiting screen time after school.

Teacher: That's a good step. Encourage reading or creative hobbies instead.

Parent: Do you recommend any apps for learning?

Teacher: Yes, but in moderation. Offline activities are better for concentration.

Parent: Thank you. We'll work on this together.

16. Parent Requesting Extra Help

Parent: My daughter wants to improve her grammar. Can you suggest something?

Teacher: Certainly! She can join our remedial English class on Thursdays.

Parent: That would be great. She's eager to improve.

Teacher: I'll also give her a few practice worksheets and vocabulary lists.

Parent: Thank you! Should we help her revise at home?

Teacher: Yes, even 20 minutes of grammar revision a day can make a big difference.

Parent: She also struggles with writing introductions.

Teacher: We'll work on that with guided writing tasks in class.

Parent: That sounds perfect.

Teacher: I appreciate her motivation. With practice, she'll show great progress.

Parent: Thank you for your support.

17. Meeting About Class Participation

Teacher: I've noticed your son is very quiet during discussions.
Parent: Yes, he's always been more of a listener.
Teacher: Listening is good, but we want to help him express his thoughts too.
Parent: How can we help him with that?
Teacher: Encourage him to express opinions during dinner conversations or book reading.
Parent: That's a great idea. He does love reading.
Teacher: He has potential. When he speaks, his points are thoughtful.
Parent: We'll encourage him without pressure.
Teacher: That's the best way. We'll also give him low-pressure speaking chances.
Parent: Thank you for being so understanding.

18. Parent Asking About Group Work

Parent: How does my child perform in group activities?
Teacher: He's respectful and listens well, but sometimes hesitates to take the lead.
Parent: He's a bit unsure of himself in front of others.
Teacher: He collaborates nicely but needs to assert his ideas more confidently.
Parent: Should we practice that at home?
Teacher: Yes. Roleplaying or encouraging leadership in chores can help.
Parent: That's a great idea.
Teacher: We also rotate group leaders, so he'll get a chance soon.
Parent: Please let us know how he responds.
Teacher: Certainly. I'll keep you updated.
Parent: Thank you for helping him grow socially.

19. Parent Concerned About Peer Pressure

Parent: My child seems influenced by her friends and imitates them.
Teacher: Peer pressure is common at this age. We do talk about it in class.
Parent: She recently started asking for things she never cared about before.
Teacher: It's important to talk openly with her about values and decision-making.
Parent: Do you notice changes in her school behavior?
Teacher: She's still respectful and attentive, but more conscious of peer opinions.
Parent: Should we worry?
Teacher: Not yet. It's part of growing up. But boundaries are essential.
Parent: We'll guide her gently.
Teacher: That's wise. If needed, she can speak to our counselor.
Parent: Thank you. That's reassuring.

20. Discussion About Language Barriers

Teacher: Your child is adjusting well, but English still poses some challenges.
Parent: We speak our mother tongue at home, so that might be affecting it.
Teacher: That's perfectly okay. Multilingual children often take time.
Parent: How can we help her improve English fluency?
Teacher: Encourage her to watch English cartoons, read picture books, and speak simple sentences.
Parent: We'll try that. Is she able to follow lessons?
Teacher: Mostly yes. She's trying hard, which is wonderful.
Parent: Thank you. We'll support her more actively.
Teacher: She's bright. A little boost at home will go a long way.
Parent: We appreciate your effort.

21. Feedback After a School Event

Parent: My son enjoyed the school annual day a lot!

Teacher: That's great to hear. He performed confidently on stage.

Parent: We were proud! It's his first time speaking in front of a crowd.

Teacher: He did wonderfully. The practice sessions helped him a lot.

Parent: Please thank the drama teacher too.

Teacher: I will. He showed great enthusiasm during rehearsals.

Parent: Do you encourage all students to take part?

Teacher: Absolutely. It builds confidence and teamwork.

Parent: We'd love him to be in more such events.

Teacher: He's welcome anytime. We love his spirit.

Parent: Thank you for creating such opportunities.

CHAPTER FIFTEEN

CONVERSATION BETWEEN THE TEACHER AND THE MANAGEMENT

1. On Student Performance

Management: How are your students performing this term?
Teacher: Overall, they are doing well. A majority of students have shown improvement since the last term.
Management: That's good. Are there any particular areas where they're facing challenges?
Teacher: Yes, a few students are struggling with grammar in English and problem-solving in Math.
Management: Have you identified the causes?
Teacher: Mostly due to lack of foundational clarity and poor study habits.
Management: How are you addressing that?
Teacher: I've started weekly remedial classes and use differentiated worksheets.
Management: Are parents involved in the follow-up?
Teacher: Yes, I regularly update them and give suggestions for home practice.
Management: That's proactive. Are you tracking progress?
Teacher: Absolutely. I maintain records and assess them bi-weekly.

Management: Excellent. Keep up the good work.

2. On Teaching Methods

Management: What teaching strategies do you use to engage your students?
Teacher: I use interactive methods—group work, quizzes, peer teaching, and real-life examples.
Management: That's good. How do you vary your approach for different learners?
Teacher: I use visuals for visual learners, oral discussion for auditory learners, and hands-on activities for kinesthetic learners.
Management: Do you follow a specific instructional model?
Teacher: Yes, I follow the "I do, we do, you do" model for gradual release of responsibility.
Management: How do you check for understanding during lessons?
Teacher: I use questioning techniques, mini-assessments, and exit slips.
Management: And how do students respond to these methods?
Teacher: They're more engaged and less passive. Participation has increased.
Management: How do you reflect on your lessons?
Teacher: I maintain a teaching journal and review feedback from students.
Management: Very thoughtful. Thank you for your dedication.

3. On Class Discipline

Management: How do you handle discipline issues in your classroom?
Teacher: I begin the year with clear expectations and classroom norms.
Management: Do you involve students in setting those norms?
Teacher: Yes. That creates ownership and mutual respect.
Management: What strategies do you use when students misbehave?
Teacher: I use positive reinforcement, redirection, and if needed, time-outs or reflection sheets.
Management: How often do you escalate to higher authorities?

Teacher: Rarely. Most issues are resolved in class. For serious cases, I inform the coordinator.

Management: What's the overall behavior trend in your class?

Teacher: Mostly positive. Students understand boundaries and feel safe.

Management: How do you manage repeated defaulters?

Teacher: I use behavior charts and meet their parents early.

Management: Excellent. Prevention is always better than punishment.

Teacher: Exactly. A respectful environment leads to fewer issues.

4. On Student Attendance

Management: Have you noticed any attendance issues in your class?

Teacher: Yes, two students have been absent frequently this term.

Management: Have you contacted their parents?

Teacher: Yes. One had health issues; the other was unclear. I followed up twice.

Management: How does absenteeism affect their performance?

Teacher: They miss key concepts and struggle to catch up.

Management: Do you provide any support when they return?

Teacher: I give a summary lesson and peer support through notes.

Management: That's helpful. Do you report chronic absenteeism?

Teacher: Yes, I update the attendance officer weekly.

Management: Good. Consistent follow-up makes a difference.

Teacher: I also motivate regular students with perfect attendance recognition.

Management: Great initiative. Keep promoting consistency.

5. On Parent Communication

Management: How often do you communicate with parents?

Teacher: I follow a monthly interaction schedule and communicate as needed.

Management: What channels do you use?

Teacher: Mostly phone calls, school diary notes, and WhatsApp updates for quick messages.

Management: Do you face any communication gaps?

Teacher: Sometimes, especially if parents are unresponsive. But I try multiple times.

Management: How do parents generally respond to your feedback?

Teacher: Most are cooperative. A few need more convincing.

Management: Do you inform them only about problems?

Teacher: No, I also share positive feedback to maintain balance.

Management: That's excellent. How do you handle sensitive conversations?

Teacher: I speak respectfully and focus on solutions, not just issues.

Management: Great approach. Please document major interactions.

Teacher: Certainly. I log every major discussion in my communication file.

6. *On Use of Technology*

Management: How do you integrate technology into your teaching?

Teacher: I regularly use PowerPoint, online quizzes, and short educational videos in my lessons.

Management: That's good. Are students comfortable with digital tools?

Teacher: Yes, most students are quite familiar. For those who struggle, I give simple guidance.

Management: Do you use online platforms for assignments or assessments?

Teacher: Yes, I sometimes use Google Forms for formative assessments and to track understanding.

Management: How do you ensure that technology enhances, not distracts?

Teacher: I use it with purpose. I always set clear objectives for any digital activity.

Management: Do you face technical challenges?

Teacher: Occasionally, like internet glitches, but I always keep a backup plan.

Management: That's responsible. Have you explored any new apps or tools?

Teacher: Recently, I started using Quizizz and Padlet to increase student engagement.

Management: Excellent. Please share useful tools with your peers.

Teacher: Certainly. I'll prepare a small resource list for the staff room board.

7. On Assessment Methods

Management: How do you assess your students' progress?

Teacher: I use a combination of class tests, oral questioning, project work, and observation.

Management: Do you use any specific format for feedback?

Teacher: Yes, I maintain a rubric-based checklist for writing and project tasks.

Management: How often do you conduct formal assessments?

Teacher: Twice a month for minor assessments and once every term for summative evaluations.

Management: How do students respond to your assessment methods?

Teacher: They find them fair and structured. Rubrics help them understand expectations.

Management: How do you handle students who underperform?

Teacher: I give individual feedback and arrange extra practice assignments.

Management: Do you track growth over time?

Teacher: Yes. I compare their term-to-term scores and note behavioral patterns.

Management: Excellent. Continuous monitoring is key.

Teacher: Agreed. It helps tailor my teaching to student needs.

8. On Handling Weak Students

Management: How do you support students who are falling behind?

Teacher: I identify them through assessments and then modify lessons to suit their pace.

Management: Do you conduct remedial classes?

Teacher: Yes, twice a week during zero periods for core subjects.

Management: How do you track their improvement?

Teacher: I maintain a remedial file with pre- and post-assessment scores.

Management: Do you involve their parents in the process?

Teacher: Definitely. I meet them monthly to review progress and give home-based suggestions.

Management: What kind of challenges do you face?

Teacher: Some students lack parental support or motivation, which delays improvement.

Management: How do you tackle that?

Teacher: I offer peer support groups and praise small improvements to build confidence.

Management: Great strategy. Do you coordinate with the counselor if needed?

Teacher: Yes. I refer students showing signs of emotional distress or learning barriers.

Management: Thank you. Your commitment makes a big difference.

9. On Involvement in Co-Curricular Activities

Management: Are you actively involved in co-curricular programs?

Teacher: Yes. I mentor the Literary Club and also help coordinate competitions.

Management: That's wonderful. Do you find it helps build student-teacher rapport?

Teacher: Absolutely. Students open up more outside the classroom environment.

Management: How do you balance this with academic responsibilities?

Teacher: I plan ahead and delegate small tasks to student leaders for better time management.

Management: What kind of events have you helped organize?

Teacher: Debates, elocution, art contests, and inter-house quiz competitions.

Management: Do students benefit from these programs?

Teacher: Yes. They develop leadership, confidence, and team spirit.

Management: How do you identify student talents?

Teacher: Through classroom observation and encouraging voluntary participation.

Management: Keep it up. Co-curriculars are vital for holistic education.

Teacher: I completely agree. I enjoy being a part of these activities.

10. On Professional Development

Management: Have you attended any workshops or training recently?

Teacher: Yes. I attended a faculty development program on NEP implementation last month.

Management: That's excellent. What was your key takeaway?

Teacher: The emphasis on experiential learning and competency-based education stood out.

Management: Have you applied those ideas in your class?

Teacher: Yes. I now use more real-world scenarios in lesson activities.

Management: Do you share your learning with peers?

Teacher: Yes. I presented a short session during our staff meeting.

Management: That's commendable. Any plans to attend more sessions?

Teacher: I'm enrolled for an upcoming webinar on inclusive classrooms next week.

Management: Very good. Please encourage your colleagues to register too.

Teacher: I'll do that. Continuous learning helps all of us grow professionally.

11. On Syllabus Completion

Management: Are you on schedule with the syllabus this term?

Teacher: Yes, I follow a weekly planner and update it regularly. So far, I'm exactly on track.

Management: That's good. Do you include time for revision?

Teacher: Yes, I've allocated the last two weeks of the term specifically for revisions and sample test practice.

Management: Do you use any tracking method for lesson completion?

Teacher: I mark every completed lesson in the curriculum plan and also maintain a soft copy for sharing.

Management: Have you faced any delays so far?

Teacher: Minor ones due to holidays, but I compensated with extra worksheets and flipped classroom tasks.

Management: Do you adjust pace depending on class understanding?

Teacher: Absolutely. For complex topics, I slow down and use two periods instead of one.

Management: What about students who are absent during key lessons?

Teacher: I conduct catch-up sessions and provide notes via class group.

Management: That's efficient. Continue maintaining structured records.

Teacher: Thank you. I ensure both pace and quality are balanced.

12. On Exam Preparedness

Management: Are your students ready for the upcoming exams?

Teacher: Yes, we've been revising since last week. I've covered all key areas in class.

Management: Have you conducted any mock tests?

Teacher: Yes, we had two already. I analyze the results to see where students need help.

Management: Are you seeing improvement in weak performers?

Teacher: Yes, especially those attending the remedial classes. They're gaining confidence.

Management: Do you share revision plans with students?

Teacher: Definitely. I post weekly revision topics on the board and on the class group.

Management: How do you keep students motivated?

Teacher: I give daily revision challenges and reward consistent effort.

Management: What support do parents provide during this period?

Teacher: I briefed them during the last PTM. Most are ensuring a distraction-free environment at home.

Management: Very good. Be sure to avoid last-minute rush.

Teacher: Yes. I always complete core content at least a week before exams.

13. On Teacher's Role in School Culture

Management: How do you contribute to building a positive school environment?

Teacher: I promote values like respect, teamwork, and responsibility in daily classroom interactions.

Management: That's great. Do students respond well to that?

Teacher: Yes, they feel heard and respected, which improves behavior and attitude.

Management: Do you collaborate with fellow teachers on initiatives?

Teacher: I work with the discipline committee and help with student council training.

Management: That's commendable. How do you handle conflicts among students?

Teacher: I facilitate open discussions and restorative conversations. It helps resolve misunderstandings.

Management: Do you celebrate student achievements?

Teacher: Yes. I display student work and recognize effort in class regularly.

Management: These small actions matter. Any suggestions to improve staff morale?

Teacher: Maybe more informal sharing sessions or appreciation circles.

Management: Good idea. Let's discuss that with the staff.

Teacher: I'd be happy to support such initiatives.

14. On Documentation and Reporting

Management: Are your academic records up to date?

Teacher: Yes, I maintain digital and physical files for attendance, grades, and lesson plans.

Management: How frequently do you update them?

Teacher: Attendance is updated daily, grades after every assessment, and lesson plans weekly.

Management: Do you use the school's LMS for reporting?

Teacher: Yes, I upload student marks and remarks on the portal regularly.

Management: Have parents been accessing it?

Teacher: Most do. I guide those who face difficulties with login.

Management: That's helpful. How do you manage documentation during busy periods?

Teacher: I set fixed weekly slots for documentation to avoid last-minute stress.

Management: That's a good practice. Do you back up your files?

Teacher: Yes, I keep a Google Drive copy and also sync with the school server.

Management: Very systematic. Please support new teachers with this as well.

Teacher: Absolutely. I've already shared my template with two new staff members.

15. On Feedback and Professional Growth

Management: Do you reflect on your teaching practices regularly?

Teacher: Yes, I reflect weekly and note down what worked and what didn't in a journal.

Management: Do you seek feedback from students?

Teacher: Informally, yes. I sometimes ask them what they liked or found confusing in the lesson.

Management: That's excellent. Have you made any changes based on their feedback?

Teacher: Yes. For example, I started using more real-life examples in science after students asked for practical relevance.

Management: Have you received feedback from peers?

Teacher: Yes, during peer observations. It helped improve my questioning strategies.

Management: Are you open to class observations by coordinators?

Teacher: Definitely. I believe feedback helps me grow as a teacher.

Management: Have you set any personal development goals this year?

Teacher: Yes. I want to enhance my ICT skills and learn basic video editing for flipped classroom content.

Management: That's a great goal. Keep developing professionally.

Teacher: Thank you. I appreciate the school's support and encouragement.

16. On Handling Emergencies

Management: Have you been trained in handling school emergencies?

Teacher: Yes, I've attended the school's fire drill, first aid workshop, and basic safety training.

Management: If a student suddenly faints in class, what would you do?

Teacher: First, I'd check for responsiveness, then immediately inform the nurse and school office.

Management: Good. Do you know where emergency numbers are displayed?

Teacher: Yes, we have a copy on the noticeboard and inside the staff room.

Management: Have you dealt with any real emergencies before?

Teacher: Once, a student had a nosebleed during class. I calmly assisted and sent him to the clinic.

Management: That's reassuring. How do you ensure safety during field trips?

Teacher: I conduct a headcount regularly, keep emergency kits, and maintain contact with all staff.

Management: Excellent. Are you confident in managing a lockdown or evacuation?

Teacher: Yes. I brief my students about procedures and keep them calm during drills.

Management: Preparedness is key. Please help new teachers stay updated too.

Teacher: Of course. I'll share my notes with them.

17. On Inclusive Education

Management: How do you support students with special learning needs in your class?

Teacher: I use simplified instructions, visual aids, and give them extra time when needed.

Management: Have you received training in inclusive practices?

Teacher: I attended a workshop last term on teaching strategies for neurodiverse students.

Management: Do you work with the school counselor?

Teacher: Yes, especially for students with anxiety, ADHD, or mild dyslexia.

Management: How do you maintain confidentiality and sensitivity?

Teacher: I never label or isolate them. I treat them equally and focus on strengths.

Management: That's important. Do parents appreciate your efforts?

Teacher: Most do. I stay in regular touch and provide practical tips for home support.

Management: Are your lesson plans inclusive?

Teacher: I try to use multi-sensory methods and flexible assessments for everyone.

Management: Very good. Inclusive teaching benefits all students.

Teacher: I agree. Every learner deserves dignity and opportunity.

18. On Mentoring Junior Teachers

Management: Do you mentor any of the newer teachers?

Teacher: Yes, I've been paired with two teachers for subject support and classroom management guidance.

Management: How often do you meet them?

Teacher: We meet every Friday after school to reflect on challenges and plan lessons.

Management: Do they find your guidance useful?

Teacher: They've said so. I also observe their classes occasionally and provide feedback.

Management: That's great. Do you share your teaching resources with them?

Teacher: Absolutely. I share my digital notes, activity templates, and assessment rubrics.

Management: How do you help them during stressful periods?

Teacher: I encourage time management, prioritization, and positive student interactions.

Management: Are you documenting your mentoring process?

Teacher: Yes. I maintain a simple logbook and submit monthly summaries.

Management: That's excellent leadership.

Teacher: Thank you. I enjoy supporting peers—it helps me grow too.

19. On Teacher Stress and Well-being

Management: How are you managing your workload and well-being this year?

Teacher: I've started organizing tasks weekly and taking breaks between classes. It's helping.

Management: Have you felt overwhelmed recently?

Teacher: During exam season, yes. But I delegate student duties like paper collection and board writing.

Management: That's smart. Do you have a support group among staff?

Teacher: Yes, we have a WhatsApp group where we share tips and vent politely. It really helps.

Management: Have you used the school counselor services?

Teacher: Once. I had a helpful discussion about managing work-life boundaries.

Management: Excellent. Do you practice any self-care habits?

Teacher: Yes. I do short breathing exercises and maintain a gratitude journal.

Management: That's great to hear.

Teacher: I also reduce screen time after 7 p.m. for better sleep.

Management: Please share these techniques during our staff wellness day.

Teacher: I'd be glad to. Mental health matters in teaching too.

20. On Innovation in the Classroom

Management: Have you tried any new or creative teaching methods recently?

Teacher: Yes, I conducted a "flipped classroom" session where students prepared and taught short topics.

Management: That's wonderful. How did students respond?

Teacher: They were excited and felt empowered. It increased participation.

Management: Have you used project-based learning?

Teacher: Yes. In Social Science, I had students create mock village plans to learn about local governance.

Management: Very innovative. Do you share these ideas with peers?

Teacher: I presented this strategy at our last teacher circle meeting.

Management: What motivates you to try new ideas?

Teacher: I want to make learning memorable and relevant. Repetition bores both students and teachers.

Management: How do you measure success?

Teacher: Through student enthusiasm, improved application, and feedback forms.

Management: Excellent. Keep leading by example.

Teacher: Thank you. I believe innovation starts with small experiments.

WAYS TO APPRECIATE STUDENTS

Simple & Classic Alternatives

1. Excellent!
2. Great job!
3. Well done!
4. Fantastic!
5. Brilliant!
6. Wonderful!
7. Superb!
8. That's amazing!
9. Nice work!
10. Outstanding!

Positive & Personal Praise

1. I'm proud of you!
2. That's a huge improvement!
3. You've really outdone yourself!
4. You've made me smile!
5. That shows dedication!

6. You're learning so well!
7. You're on the right track!
8. You've nailed it!
9. That was impressive!
10. You gave it your best!

Encouraging Growth & Effort

21. You've improved so much!
22. That's how it's done!
23. Look how far you've come!
24. You're really getting it!
25. You're growing stronger every day!
26. You've worked so hard on this!
27. You're making great progress!
28. That's real improvement!
29. I love how you did that!
30. You kept going — great perseverance!

Creative & Fun Praise

31. That's gold star work!
32. You're a rockstar!
33. You deserve a high-five!
34. That was top-notch!
35. You aced it!
36. That's what I call smart thinking!
37. You're shining today!
38. You made my day!
39. I love your thinking!
40. Now that's excellence in action!

Group/Classroom Praise

41. Let's give a round of applause!
42. That's a model answer!
43. Friends, take note — that's quality work!
44. You just set an example for others!
45. Keep it up — this is inspiring!
46. That's leadership right there!
47. You're raising the bar for the whole class!
48. This deserves a celebration!
49. You've earned a big thumbs-up!
50. That's learning at its best!

Verbal Praise (Simple & Powerful)

1. "Well done!"
2. "Excellent work today!"
3. "I'm proud of you!"
4. "You tried really hard — great job!"
5. "That's a smart answer."
6. "You're improving every day."
7. "I can see you gave it your best."
8. "You didn't give up — that's impressive!"
9. "That's a creative solution."
10. "You've made great progress!"

Written Appreciation (On Notebooks or Reports)

11. "Outstanding effort!"
12. "Keep up the good work."
13. "Neat and clear presentation."
14. "Well-structured answer."
15. "Excellent participation in class."
16. "Great teamwork today."
17. "Very thoughtful response."
18. "Beautiful handwriting!"
19. "You've grown a lot since last term."
20. "This is your best work yet!"

Public Praise (Class or Assembly)

21. "Let's give a round of applause for ___."
22. "___ has shown great leadership today."
23. "___ helped a friend — that's kindness in action!"
24. "Today's star student is ___."
25. "I noticed ___ stayed focused the entire time — impressive!"
26. "___ asked a great question — keep thinking critically!"
27. "___ took initiative during group work — well done!"
28. "___ showed real curiosity — that's how we learn!"
29. "___ completed every assignment with care."
30. **"___ stepped out of their comfort zone — very brave!"

Non-verbal Praise (Subtle but Effective)

31. Thumbs up
32. Applause
33. Writing "Excellent!" or "✓?✓?" on their work
34. A smile or nod of approval

35. Giving a sticker, star, or badge
36. Displaying their work on the wall or board
37. Sending a "well done" note home
38. Giving a classroom title: "Scientist of the Week" or "Grammar Guru"
39. Giving them classroom responsibility as recognition
40. Letting them lead an activity (reading aloud, checking homework)

Encouraging Phrases (Growth & Character)

41. "You're becoming more responsible."
42. "I appreciate your honesty."
43. "You handled that situation very maturely."
44. "You're a good role model for your classmates."
45. "You showed real patience today."
46. "You're learning from your mistakes — that's the right attitude."
47. "Your hard work is paying off."
48. "I admire your consistency."
49. "I appreciate your positive attitude."
50. **"You're becoming a true independent learner!"

Effort-Based Appreciation

51. "You gave it your full attention — I noticed that."
52. "You didn't give up even when it was tough. That's strength."
53. "You kept trying until you got it — excellent perseverance."
54. "Effort like yours is what leads to success."
55. "That was a tough question, but you didn't shy away from it."
56. "You're developing a great learning habit."
57. "You worked quietly and consistently — that's discipline."
58. "You asked for help when needed — that's being smart."
59. "You took responsibility for your learning."
60. **"You stayed focused the whole class — very commendable."

Creativity and Problem Solving

61. "That's such a creative idea!"
62. "You found a unique way to solve the problem — impressive."
63. "I love how you think outside the box."
64. "You used imagination beautifully here."
65. "Great use of colors and visuals!"
66. "Your project stood out for its originality."
67. "That's a very thoughtful design."
68. "You came up with a brilliant analogy."
69. "That's a solution I hadn't even thought of!"
70. **"Your creativity adds value to our classroom."

Behavior and Attitude Praise

71. "Thank you for being respectful."
72. "You listened patiently — that's maturity."
73. "You waited your turn — that's very thoughtful."
74. "You showed great manners today."
75. "I noticed you cleaned up without being asked — thank you!"
76. "You supported your friend when they needed help — very kind."
77. "Your positive energy lifts the class."
78. "You showed great self-control in a difficult moment."
79. "Thank you for setting a good example for others."
80. **"You were honest and responsible — that shows integrity."

Participation and Leadership

81. "Thank you for volunteering."

82. "You led your group very well."
83. "You included everyone in the task — great leadership!"
84. "Your confidence while speaking was inspiring."
85. "You helped your team stay organized — well done."
86. "You took initiative without being told — impressive."
87. "You handled your responsibility with care."
88. "You stayed calm under pressure — a true leader."
89. "You encouraged your teammates — good team spirit."
90. **"Your enthusiasm inspired the others."

Growth and Motivation Phrases

91. "You've come such a long way — be proud!"
92. "You've grown not just academically, but personally too."
93. "Every day, you're getting stronger at this."
94. "You're becoming more independent in your learning."
95. "You took feedback and used it to improve — fantastic!"
96. "Your journey is showing progress."
97. "Mistakes didn't stop you, you turned them into lessons."
98. "Your learning attitude is inspiring."
99. "You are building habits that will take you far."
100. "I believe in you — and now you're starting to believe in yourself."

CHAPTER SEVENTEEN

COLLOCATION

Collocation refers to the habitual combination of particular words in a language. In simpler terms, it means **which words tend to go together naturally** in English. These combinations sound "right" to native speakers, and using the wrong combinations often sounds awkward or incorrect.

Definition:

Collocation is a pair or group of words that are **often used together** in a way that sounds natural to native speakers.

Types of Collocations (with Examples):

1. **Adjective + Noun**

   - *strong coffee* (NOT **powerful coffee**)
   - *heavy rain* (NOT **strong rain**)

2. **Verb + Noun**

   - *make a decision* (NOT **do a decision**)
   - *catch a cold* (NOT **take a cold**)

3. **Noun + Noun**

   - *a piece of advice* (NOT **a bit of advice**)
   - *a surge of anger*

4. **Verb + Adverb**

- *speak fluently*
- *whisper softly*

5. **Adverb + Adjective**

- *deeply concerned*
- *highly unlikely*

6. **Verb + Preposition**

- *depend on*
- *belong to*

Why Collocations Matter:

- They **make your English sound more natural** and fluent.
- They help in **clear and precise communication.**
- Native speakers use collocations without thinking—they're part of **natural speech and writing.**

Verb + noun collocations:

1. make a decision
She made a difficult decision about her career.
2. do homework
The children did their homework after school.
3. take a break
Let's take a short break before we continue.
4. give advice
He gave me excellent advice.
5. catch a cold
She caught a cold during the winter.
6. save time
Using email can save a lot of time.
7. break a record
He broke the school's sprint record.
8. make an effort

You must make an effort to study daily.

9. have a rest

You should have a rest after the long trip.

10. pay attention

Please pay attention in class.

11. miss a chance

He missed a chance to impress his boss.

12. meet a deadline

We must meet the deadline by Friday.

13. lose weight

She is trying to lose weight.

14. gain experience

You will gain experience during your internship.

15. take notes

Students should take notes during the lecture.

16. make money

He wants to make money from his blog.

17. give a speech

She gave a speech at the ceremony.

18. draw a picture

The child drew a picture of a house.

19. write a letter

He wrote a letter to the principal.

20. have lunch

We had lunch at a nearby café.

21. make a mistake

Everyone makes mistakes sometimes.

22. do the dishes

I'll do the dishes after dinner.

23. lose your temper

He lost his temper during the meeting.

24. get a job

She got a job at a software company.

25. tell a story

Grandma told us a bedtime story.

... (and so on up to 100)

26. deliver a message

The boy delivered the message to the teacher.

27. start a conversation

He started a conversation with a stranger.

28. make a promise

She made a promise to call her friend every week.

29. take a photo

They took a photo of the beautiful sunset.

30. play a game

We played a game during English class.

31. keep a secret

Can you keep a secret about the surprise party?

32. make a suggestion

I'd like to make a suggestion for the project.

33. send an email

She sent an email to her professor about the assignment.

34. have an idea

I have an idea that could improve the presentation.

35. make a plan

We made a plan to meet at the library tomorrow.

36. ask a question

May I ask a question about today's lesson?

37. win a prize

He won a prize in the essay competition.

38. offer help

She offered help to her classmates during the activity.

39. receive a gift

He received a gift for his birthday.

40. take a seat

Please take a seat while you wait.

41. give an answer

Can you give an answer to the riddle?

42. have a chat

Let's have a chat after class.

43. make progress

You've made great progress in your speaking skills.

44. do business

They do business with companies around the world.

45. catch a bus

She caught a bus to college this morning.

46. ask permission

You must ask permission before using the computer.

47. break the ice

He told a funny story to break the ice.

48. close a deal

The manager closed a deal with the client.

49. hold a meeting

We will hold a meeting on Friday afternoon.

50. take a shower

He took a shower before leaving for school.

51. make an excuse

She made an excuse for coming late to class.

52. make a complaint

They made a complaint about the noisy classroom.

53. keep a diary

She keeps a diary to write her daily thoughts.

54. do a favour

Can you do me a favour and pass this note to him?

55. take a nap

I usually take a nap in the afternoon after lunch.

56. make an appointment

I made an appointment with the dentist for next week.

57. give a warning

The teacher gave a warning for late submission of work.

58. earn a living

He earns a living by teaching English online.

59. give a presentation

She gave a presentation on environmental issues.

60. get married

They got married in a small ceremony last summer.

61. have a dream

I had a strange dream last night about flying.

62. get ready

Get ready for the school trip by 8 a.m.

63. make a call

She made a call to confirm the appointment.

64. do research

He is doing research on language acquisition.

65. run a business

Her father runs a small clothing business.

66. give permission

The principal gave permission to use the hall.

67. have fun

We had fun playing outdoor games.

68. get dressed

He got dressed quickly for the online class.

69. make a reservation

I made a reservation at the hotel for next weekend.

70. catch a glimpse

I caught a glimpse of the rainbow before it disappeared.

71. give someone a ride

Can you give me a ride to the bus stop?

72. keep in touch

Let's keep in touch after graduation.

73. lose interest

He lost interest in the book halfway through.

74. make a list

She made a list of groceries to buy.

75. take a look

Take a look at this amazing artwork!

76. get a haircut

He got a haircut before the interview.

77. have a look

Have a look at these notes — they're helpful.

78. do your best

Don't worry about the result — just do your best.

79. make a request

I'd like to make a request for extra time.

80. do the shopping

She did the shopping early in the morning.

81. give someone a hand

Can you give me a hand with this project?

82. keep quiet

Please keep quiet while the exam is going on.

83. lose hope

Never lose hope, even when things are tough.

84. take action

We must take action to protect the environment.

85. get lost

We got lost on the way to the museum.

86. catch fire

The kitchen caught fire due to a short circuit.

87. make an effort

You need to make an effort to improve your grades.

88. make a difference

One kind act can make a big difference.

89. have patience

You must have patience when learning a new language.

90. keep a promise

He always keeps his promises.

91. pay a visit

We paid a visit to our grandparents last weekend.

92. gain knowledge

Reading books helps us gain knowledge.

93. take responsibility

She took responsibility for the group's failure.

94. have confidence

You should have confidence in your abilities.

95. give feedback

The teacher gave valuable feedback on our essays.

96. get the job done

We stayed late to get the job done.

97. do the cleaning

I do the cleaning every weekend at home.

98. make a fortune

He made a fortune selling handmade crafts.

99. pass an exam

She passed the exam with flying colors.

100. take part

They took part in the school play.

Adjective + Noun Collocations

1. strong coffee

He needs a cup of strong coffee every morning.

2. heavy rain

Heavy rain caused the match to be postponed.

3. bright future

She has a bright future ahead.

4. deep sleep

After a long day, he went into deep sleep.

5. loud noise

The loud noise from the construction site was disturbing.

6. serious problem

Pollution is a serious problem in many cities.

7. great success

Her presentation was a great success.

8. hard work

Nothing beats hard work and dedication.

9. fast car

He drives a fast car.

10. strong opinion

She has strong opinions on education.

11. quick response

The police gave a quick response.

12. cold weather

Cold weather can be dangerous without proper clothing.

13. hot meal

A hot meal was ready when he got home.

14. big mistake

Leaving your keys in the car was a big mistake.

15. soft voice

She spoke in a soft voice.

16. clear sky

The sky was clear and blue.

17. serious injury

He suffered a serious injury during the game.

18. rich man

He became a rich man through business.

19. tall building

They live in a tall building.

20. old friend

I met an old friend at the bookstore.

21. happy ending

The movie had a happy ending.

22. sad story

It was a sad story about lost love.

23. full moon

We went hiking under the full moon.

24. hard question

That was a hard question to answer.

25. new job

She started a new job last week.

26. blue sky

The blue sky stretched endlessly.

27. busy street

The busy street was filled with cars.

28. beautiful dress

She wore a beautiful dress to the party.

29. young child

The young child ran into the room.

30. poor performance

The team had a poor performance.

31. important decision

That was an important decision for the company.

32. early morning

I wake up early every morning.

33. fresh air

Let's go outside and get some fresh air.

34. empty room

The empty room echoed with each step.

35. sharp knife

Be careful with that sharp knife.

36. dirty clothes

Put your dirty clothes in the laundry basket.

37. clean water

Access to clean water is a basic right.

38. green grass

The green grass was wet with dew.

39. cold drink

He asked for a cold drink.

40. sweet smile

She greeted us with a sweet smile.

41. tough decision

It was a tough decision to make.

42. narrow road

The car drove down a narrow road.

43. strong wind

The strong wind knocked over the fence.

44. high price

The high price stopped me from buying it.

45. low salary

She left the job because of the low salary.

46. heavy bag

He carried a heavy bag to school.

47. modern building

The campus has many modern buildings.

48. ancient temple

They visited an ancient temple in the hills.

49. short break

We took a short break before continuing.

50. long journey

It was a long journey to the village.

51. friendly face

He welcomed us with a friendly face.

52. gentle breeze

A gentle breeze blew through the trees.

53. warm welcome

We received a warm welcome at the hotel.

54. hot day

It was a hot day in summer.

55. delicious food

We enjoyed delicious food at the restaurant.

56. happy child

The happy child played in the park.

57. bright light

The bright light hurt my eyes.

58. quiet place

We found a quiet place to relax.

59. noisy crowd

The noisy crowd cheered loudly.

60. thin book

It's a thin book with only 60 pages.

61. thick blanket

He covered himself with a thick blanket.

62. simple answer

It was a simple answer to a simple question.

63. clear voice

She spoke in a clear voice.

64. white shirt

He wore a white shirt and black trousers.

65. black shoes

Her black shoes matched her bag.

66. small house

They live in a small house near the beach.

67. huge building

The city has many huge buildings.

68. open window

The open window let in fresh air.

69. closed door

He knocked on the closed door.

70. fast train

The fast train left at 6 a.m.

71. slow internet

The slow internet annoyed everyone.

72. sharp pencil

Use a sharp pencil for drawing.

73. blunt knife

The blunt knife couldn't cut the bread.

74. beautiful view

The mountain offers a beautiful view.

75. heavy traffic

We were delayed by heavy traffic.

76. calm sea

The calm sea was perfect for boating.

77. rough road

The rough road damaged the tires.

78. bright color

She chose a dress with a bright color.

79. dull movie

The movie was dull and uninteresting.

80. cool breeze

A cool breeze made the evening pleasant.

81. hot soup

The hot soup burned his tongue.

82. easy task

It was an easy task to complete.

83. difficult job

Teaching young children is a difficult job.

84. brave soldier

The brave soldier was awarded a medal.

85. lazy student

The lazy student failed the test.

86. curious mind

A curious mind always asks questions.

87. creative idea

She had a creative idea for the project.

88. long line

There was a long line at the counter.

89. short speech

He gave a short speech.

90. large room

They booked a large room for the party.

91. tiny insect

A tiny insect crawled on the table.

92. happy family

They are a happy family.

93. sad face

He had a sad face after losing the game.

94. big surprise

Her arrival was a big surprise.

95. final exam

She studied hard for the final exam.

96. quick meal
We had a quick meal before the show.
97. early train
I caught the early train to work.
98. late reply
Sorry for the late reply.
99. new book
I bought a new book yesterday.
100. old building
That's an old building from the 1800s.

Noun + Noun Collocations

1. language skills
Reading English newspapers can improve your language skills.
2. class teacher
Our class teacher is very kind and supportive.
3. exam stress
Many students suffer from exam stress before finals.
4. job interview
She prepared well for the job interview.
5. homework assignment
The teacher gave us a difficult homework assignment.
6. time management
Good time management is essential for exam success.
7. communication skills
Group discussions help develop communication skills.
8. school bag
He forgot his school bag at home.
9. traffic jam
We were late because of a traffic jam.
10. coffee shop
They met at a coffee shop near the college.
11. bus stop
There's a new bus stop near the park.
12. science project

Their science project won first prize.

13. school uniform

All students must wear the school uniform.

14. classroom environment

A positive classroom environment supports better learning.

15. computer lab

We have computer lab sessions every Wednesday.

16. sports day

The school celebrated sports day with great enthusiasm.

17. lunch break

We discussed the plan during the lunch break.

18. notice board

Your name is on the notice board.

19. school library

She borrowed a book from the school library.

20. water bottle

Don't forget to bring your water bottle to school.

21. reading habit

Parents should encourage a reading habit in children.

22. mobile phone

Students are not allowed to use mobile phones in class.

23. question paper

He submitted the question paper before time.

24. exam hall

The exam hall was silent and tense.

25. school campus

Our school campus is clean and green.

26. study material

We received the study material for the semester.

27. pen friend

I have a pen friend in Sri Lanka.

28. bus route

They changed the bus route this month.

29. lesson plan

The teacher submitted her lesson plan on Monday.

30. parent meeting

The school held a parent meeting last Friday.

31. daily routine

It's important to follow a healthy daily routine.

32. reading corner

There's a reading corner in every classroom.

33. school garden

The students take care of the school garden.

34. morning assembly

We sang the national anthem during the morning assembly.

35. group activity

The teacher arranged a group activity on climate change.

36. school bell

The school bell rang at 8:30 a.m.

37. language lab

We practice pronunciation in the language lab.

38. staff room

The teachers are having tea in the staff room.

39. class monitor

The class monitor maintains discipline in the classroom.

40. project report

We submitted the project report yesterday.

41. field trip

The class went on a field trip to the zoo.

42. science fair

Our project was selected for the science fair.

43. chalk board

The teacher wrote the answer on the chalk board.

44. class timetable

Check the class timetable on the notice board.

45. unit test

We have a unit test next Monday.

46. reading session

The reading session was quiet and focused.

47. school building

The school building was painted last summer.

48. attendance register

The teacher marked the attendance register.

49. debate competition

I participated in the school's debate competition.

50. class discussion

Today's class discussion was about pollution control.

51. school magazine

Her article was published in the school magazine.

52. sports team

He was selected for the school's sports team.

53. book fair

We visited the annual book fair last weekend.

54. school trip

The school trip to the museum was very educational.

55. class test

We had a surprise class test in mathematics.

56. writing competition

She won first place in the writing competition.

57. home task

The home task must be submitted by tomorrow.

58. school record

He broke the school record in long jump.

59. hall ticket

Don't forget to bring your hall ticket for the exam.

60. exam schedule

The exam schedule is available on the website.

61. school bag

He forgot his school bag on the bus.

62. class leader

The class leader collected the notebooks.

63. student council

The student council organized a cultural event.

64. lesson summary

She wrote a lesson summary after each class.

65. language partner

Practising with a language partner helps in fluency.

66. question session

There will be a question session after the lecture.

67. tuition fee

The tuition fee must be paid before the deadline.

68. library book

I returned the library book after two weeks.

69. class notebook

Please submit your class notebook on Monday.

70. lunch box

He forgot to bring his lunch box today.

71. group leader

Each team must have a group leader.

72. library card

You need a library card to borrow books.

73. project file

The teacher checked each student's project file.

74. exam marks

She was happy with her exam marks.

75. answer sheet

Please write neatly on your answer sheet.

76. class notes

He borrowed my class notes for revision.

77. sports uniform

We wear a different sports uniform on Wednesdays.

78. practical exam

The practical exam will be held in the lab.

79. reading material

Extra reading material is available online.

80. school anthem

The school anthem is sung during assembly.

81. study timetable

Create a study timetable to manage your subjects.

82. admission form

Fill out the admission form carefully.

83. midterm exam

The midterm exam starts next week.

84. model paper

Solve the model paper for better practice.

85. chapter summary

Each student must write a chapter summary.

86. subject teacher

The subject teacher explained the concept clearly.

87. learning outcome

Reading aloud improved their learning outcome.

88. computer class

Our computer class is on Fridays.

89. text book

The text book has colourful illustrations.

90. group work

Group work encourages teamwork and cooperation.

91. answer key

The answer key will be given after the test.

92. debate team

He is the captain of the school's debate team.

93. essay topic

The essay topic was on 'My Role Model'.

94. assignment submission

Today is the last date for assignment submission.

95. chalk box

The teacher asked for a new chalk box.

96. study group

We formed a study group for the final exams.

97. question bank

He revised all questions from the question bank.

98. school auditorium

The play was staged in the school auditorium.

99. notice period

You must give a notice period before leaving.

100. science teacher

Our science teacher gave a demonstration on electricity.

Verb + Preposition Collocations

1. agree with

I agree with your opinion.

2. apologize for

She apologized for being late.

3. apply for

He applied for a new job.

4. approve of

The manager approved of her suggestion.

5. believe in

I believe in lifelong learning.
6. belong to
This book belongs to the library.
7. care for
She cares for her grandmother.
8. comment on
The teacher commented on my essay.
9. complain about
They complained about the noise.
10. concentrate on
You need to concentrate on your studies.
11. confide in
She confided in her best friend.
12. conform to
You must conform to the school rules.
13. consent to
He consented to the terms of the agreement.
14. cope with
She copes well with pressure.
15. deal with
He deals with customer complaints.
16. depend on
Children depend on their parents.
17. disagree with
I disagree with your opinion.
18. dream about
Last night I dreamt about the ocean.
19. escape from
The prisoner escaped from jail.
20. explain to
He explained the problem to the teacher.
21. feel like
I feel like going for a walk.
22. focus on
You should focus on your goals.
23. forgive for
Please forgive me for the mistake.
24. get rid of

We need to get rid of the clutter.

25. hear about

Did you hear about the news?

26. insist on

She insisted on paying the bill.

27. interfere with

Don't interfere with their conversation.

28. laugh at

They laughed at the joke.

29. listen to

Listen to your teacher carefully.

30. look after

She looks after her baby brother.

31. look at

Look at the board, please.

32. look for

I'm looking for my keys.

33. object to

They objected to the proposal.

34. participate in

He participated in the race.

35. pay for

I paid for the coffee.

36. pray for

We prayed for peace.

37. prepare for

She is preparing for the exam.

38. prevent from

The rain prevented us from going out.

39. protect from

A hat protects you from the sun.

40. provide for

Parents provide for their children.

41. recover from

He recovered from his illness.

42. refer to

She referred to the textbook.

43. rely on

You can rely on me.
44. remind of
This song reminds me of my childhood.
45. resign from
She resigned from her job.
46. respond to
He responded to the email.
47. search for
I searched for the missing file.
48. suffer from
He suffers from back pain.
49. talk about
Let's talk about your project.
50. think about
I'm thinking about our vacation.
51. wait for
Please wait for your turn.
52. worry about
Don't worry about the exam results.
53. write to
She wrote to her grandmother last week.
54. argue with
He argued with his friend about the match.
55. shout at
The coach shouted at the players during practice.
56. smile at
The baby smiled at her mother.
57. speak to
You need to speak to your teacher.
58. travel to
They travelled to Paris during the holidays.
59. vote for
I voted for the best candidate.
60. work on
She is working on her science project.
61. agree on
They agreed on the terms of the contract.
62. apologize to

I apologized to my classmate for the misunderstanding.

63. belong in

This book belongs in the reference section.

64. care about

She cares deeply about animal rights.

65. charge with

He was charged with theft.

66. compare to

The teacher compared the two poems to each other.

67. compete with

Our team competed with five other schools.

68. connect to

The printer is connected to the computer.

69. contribute to

Everyone contributed to the group project.

70. crash into

The car crashed into the tree.

71. deal in

They deal in handmade crafts.

72. devote to

She devoted her life to teaching.

73. differ from

His opinion differs from mine.

74. escape into

The cat escaped into the garden.

75. fall into

He fell into the river while fishing.

76. fight for

They fought for their freedom.

77. fill with

She filled the bottle with water.

78. interact with

Students often interact with each other during group work.

79. invest in

He invested in a new start-up company.

80. introduce to

Let me introduce you to my colleague.

81. invite to

She invited me to her birthday party.

82. laugh about

We laughed about our childhood memories.

83. learn from

We learn from our mistakes.

84. leave for

They left for the airport early in the morning.

85. listen for

Listen for the announcement on the loudspeaker.

86. long for

She longed for a peaceful life in the countryside.

87. object against

They objected against the rule change.

88. prevent against

This vaccine helps prevent against infection.

89. recover after

He recovered quickly after surgery.

90. rescue from

The firefighter rescued the puppy from the fire.

91. respond with

He responded with a smile.

92. succeed in

She succeeded in passing the final exam.

93. talk to

Talk to your parents if you're feeling worried.

94. throw at

He threw the ball at his friend playfully.

95. translate into

The poem was translated into French.

96. wait on

The waiter waited on the guests politely.

97. warn about

The teacher warned us about plagiarism.

98. worry for

She worries for her brother when he travels alone.

99. check into

They checked into the hotel late at night.

100. argue about

They argued about which movie to watch.

101. account for

He couldn't account for the missing documents.

102. adhere to

All students must adhere to the school rules.

103. admit to

She admitted to breaking the vase.

104. advocate for

They advocate for children's rights.

105. argue for

He argued for better facilities in the library.

106. beg for

The child begged for a new toy.

107. boast about

He boasted about his achievements.

108. cater to

The restaurant caters to all dietary needs.

109. collaborate with

The team collaborated with engineers from another company.

110. collide with

The bike collided with a car.

111. comment about

She commented about the changes in policy.

112. communicate with

We communicate with our clients via email.

113. comply with

You must comply with the exam regulations.

114. confront with

He was confronted with new evidence.

115. connect with

She easily connects with new people.

116. consist of

The test consists of multiple-choice questions.

117. convince of

He convinced me of his innocence.

118. contribute towards

They contributed towards the school fund.

119. coordinate with

She coordinated with volunteers to arrange the event.

120. distract from

Noise can distract students from their work.

121. distinguish between

It's important to distinguish between facts and opinions.

122. engage in

The students engaged in a debate.

123. escape from

The thief escaped from the police.

124. experiment with

The scientist experimented with new materials.

125. face up to

He must face up to his responsibilities.

126. fall out with

She fell out with her best friend.

127. fill in for

Can you fill in for me at the meeting?

128. get away with

He got away with cheating in the test.

129. give in to

She gave in to the pressure from her peers.

130. hear from

I hope to hear from you soon.

131. hold on to

He held on to his beliefs strongly.

132. include in

Please include this topic in the syllabus.

133. infer from

What can we infer from this report?

134. intervene in

The teacher had to intervene in the argument.

135. lead to

Lack of sleep can lead to poor performance.

136. listen to

Always listen to your elders.

137. object to

They objected to the new rule.

138. opt for

She opted for the science stream.

139. participate in

Many students participated in the event.

140. pray to

He prayed to God for guidance.

141. prevent from

The lock prevents the door from opening.

142. provide with

The school provided students with free textbooks.

143. react to

She reacted to the news with surprise.

144. refer back to

You can refer back to the notes during revision.

145. relate to

I can relate to your experience.

146. remind about

Remind me about the meeting tomorrow.

147. report on

The journalist reported on the fire incident.

148. result in

Carelessness can result in accidents.

149. run into

I ran into an old friend yesterday.

150. see to

I'll see to the arrangements.

151. send for

We had to send for the doctor immediately.

152. separate from

Please separate the blue files from the red ones.

153. settle for

She settled for a second-hand car instead of a new one.

154. shout for

He shouted for help when he saw the fire.

155. sign up for

I signed up for a yoga class.

156. stand for

UNESCO stands for United Nations Educational, Scientific and Cultural Organization.

157. stick to
Let's stick to the original plan.

158. subscribe to
She subscribed to an online learning platform.

159. succeed at
He succeeded at his first job interview.

160. suffer with
He suffers with severe headaches.

161. take care of
She takes care of her younger siblings.

162. take part in
Many students took part in the science exhibition.

163. talk with
He talked with his friend about the issue.

164. think of
I'm thinking of a solution to the problem.

165. translate from
This book was translated from Spanish to English.

166. trust in
We must trust in our abilities.

167. turn into
The story turned into a mystery.

168. vote against
Many voted against the proposal.

169. wait upon
The servants waited upon the guests politely.

170. warn against
Doctors warn against smoking.

171. work for
He works for a multinational company.

172. write about
She wrote about her summer vacation.

173. back out of
He backed out of the agreement at the last minute.

174. base on
The film is based on a true story.

175. believe about
What do you believe about life on other planets?

176. blame for
She blamed him for the accident.
177. border on
That kind of behavior borders on rudeness.
178. bring up
She brought up an interesting point during the meeting.
179. bump into
I bumped into an old teacher yesterday.
180. call for
This situation calls for urgent action.
181. call off
They called off the event due to rain.
182. care for
Would you care for some tea?
183. carry on with
Please carry on with your work.
184. catch up with
I need to catch up with my classmates.
185. check on
He went to check on the baby.
186. come across
I came across a beautiful poem in the library.
187. come down with
She came down with the flu last week.
188. comment about
He commented about the new syllabus.
189. congratulate on
She congratulated me on my success.
190. deal with
The manager deals with all customer issues.
191. delight in
She delights in helping others.
192. depart from
The train departed from platform 4.
193. devote oneself to
He devoted himself to research.
194. dine on
We dined on local delicacies.

195. engage with

The speaker engaged well with the audience.

196. escape from

The deer escaped from the forest fire.

197. expand into

The company is expanding into new markets.

198. fall for

He fell for her immediately.

199. fill out

Please fill out this application form.

200. focus upon

We need to focus upon practical learning.

201. get on with

Let's get on with the lesson.

202. give up on

She never gave up on her dreams.

203. go along with

I'll go along with your suggestion.

204. go back to

He went back to his hometown after college.

205. grow up in

She grew up in a small village.

206. hand over to

He handed the responsibility over to his colleague.

207. help with

Can you help me with my homework?

208. hold out for

They held out for a better offer.

209. hurry up with

Please hurry up with the assignment.

210. interfere in

Don't interfere in their private matters.

211. join in on

Would you like to join in on the game?

212. keep away from

Keep away from electrical appliances when wet.

213. keep up with

It's hard to keep up with the fast-paced class.

214. knock on

He knocked on the door three times.

215. laugh with

We laughed with joy after winning the match.

216. leave out of

Why did you leave me out of the group?

217. line up for

They lined up for tickets.

218. listen in on

She listened in on their conversation secretly.

219. live with

He lives with his grandparents.

220. look down on

Don't look down on people because of their background.

221. look forward to

I'm looking forward to the weekend.

222. look into

The principal promised to look into the issue.

223. make up for

He worked hard to make up for his mistakes.

224. mix up with

I mixed up your file with someone else's.

225. move on to

Let's move on to the next topic.

226. object to

They objected to the noisy construction.

227. open up to

She finally opened up to her friend.

228. pass on to

Please pass this message on to your teacher.

229. pay attention to

Students must pay attention to the instructions.

230. point at

The teacher pointed at the board.

231. provide for

Parents work hard to provide for their children.

232. pull into

The train pulled into the station late.

233. put up with

I can't put up with the noise anymore.

234. reach out to

The counsellor reached out to the student in need.

235. remind about

Remind me about the project tomorrow.

236. report to

You must report to the office by 9 a.m.

237. reside in

She resides in a small apartment in the city.

238. result from

His illness resulted from poor hygiene.

239. run away from

The dog ran away from the fireworks.

240. run out of

We've run out of paper.

241. search through

I searched through all the drawers but found nothing.

242. send out to

They sent the invitations out to all parents.

243. set out for

They set out for the mountains early in the morning.

244. settle down in

They settled down in Canada last year.

245. show up for

He didn't show up for the rehearsal.

246. speak up for

She spoke up for her classmates in front of the principal.

247. stand up for

We should stand up for what's right.

248. stick with

Stick with your plan even if it's tough.

249. talk back to

Don't talk back to your elders.

250. think back on

I often think back on my school days.

251. throw out of

He was thrown out of the library for making noise.

252. tie to

Success is often tied to consistent effort.

253. turn away from

She turned away from the rude comment.

254. turn back from

They turned back from the hiking trail due to rain.

255. vouch for

I can vouch for her honesty.

256. walk away from

He walked away from the fight to avoid trouble.

257. wake up to

We woke up to the sound of birds chirping.

258. warn of

The sign warned of falling rocks.

259. watch over

The teacher watched over the students during the exam.

260. work out with

I work out with my friend every morning.

261. zoom in on

The photographer zoomed in on the butterfly.

262. break in on

He broke in on their conversation to give news.

263. bring about through

The reforms were brought about through public demand.

264. call out for

The child called out for her mother.

265. calm down after

He calmed down after drinking water.

266. check up on

I checked up on my grandmother yesterday.

267. come down on

The teacher came down on the students for cheating.

268. come up with

She came up with a brilliant idea.

269. cut down on

Try to cut down on junk food.

270. do away with

We should do away with outdated rules.

271. drop in o

We dropped in on our aunt without notice.

272. drop out of

He dropped out of college after the first year.

273. face up with

She had to face up with the truth.

274. fall behind in

He fell behind in his studies after the illness.

275. fill in on

Can you fill me in on what happened yesterday?

276. get around to

I'll get around to calling her tonight.

277. give in to

He gave in to the temptation of sweets.

278. go in for

She went in for engineering studies.

279. hand in to

Hand in your assignments to the front desk.

280. hold out on

Don't hold out on me — tell me everything!

281. keep out of

Keep out of the restricted area.

282. look out for

Look out for spelling mistakes.

283. make away with

The thief made away with the jewels.

284. meet up with

We met up with our cousins at the mall.

285. move in with

He moved in with his grandparents last year.

286. own up to

He owned up to breaking the vase.

287. pick on

The older kids used to pick on him at school.

288. point out to

She pointed out the error to her teacher.

289. pull out of

They pulled out of the competition due to illness.

290. read up on
I'm reading up on ancient civilizations.
291. rule out of
They ruled him out of the finals due to injury.
292. run away with
The dog ran away with the slipper.
293. run over by
He was almost run over by a bike.
294. set off for
We set off for the hill station early in the morning.
295. sign in at
Please sign in at the reception desk.
296. slow down on
You should slow down on your caffeine intake.
297. stand out from
Her painting stood out from the rest.
298. stick to
Always stick to the facts.
299. tag along with
My little brother tagged along with me to the store.
300. think over
I need time to think over your proposal.
301. tip over into
The glass tipped over into the sink.
302. tune in to
He tuned in to the radio program at 8 p.m.
303. venture into
They ventured into the jungle despite warnings.
304. wake up from
He woke up from a deep sleep.
305. weigh in on
The professor weighed in on the discussion.
306. win over with
She won them over with her charm.
307. withdraw from
He withdrew from the competition due to illness.
308. zoom out from
The drone zoomed out from the building.

309. yell at

The coach yelled at the players after the loss.

310. zone out during

She zoned out during the long lecture.

311. attend to

The nurse attended to the patient quickly.

312. bargain for

They didn't bargain for such heavy traffic.

313. break away from

He broke away from the group during the tour.

314. bring down on

The scandal brought shame down on the entire company.

315. build up to

The tension built up to a dramatic ending.

316. call in on

We called in on our aunt while passing by.

317. calm down with

She calmed down with a cup of tea.

318. check in at

Please check in at the hotel counter.

319. cheer up with

He cheered up with some good news.

320. chip in for

Everyone chipped in for the farewell gift.

321. come out of

She came out of the room crying.

322. count against

Lack of punctuality may count against you.

323. crack down on

The police cracked down on illegal parking.

324. creep up on

The deadline crept up on us.

325. cut out from

She was cut out from the final team list.

326. draw back from

He drew back from making the final decision.

327. drift off to

I drifted off to sleep during the lecture.

328. eat out at

We ate out at a local restaurant.

329. ease off on

The teacher eased off on the homework load.

330. engage with

The students engaged well with the activity.

331. fall out over

They fell out over a silly argument.

332. fill up with

The bottle filled up with rainwater.

333. follow through on

She followed through on her promise.

334. get back at

He got back at them with a clever prank.

335. glance at

She glanced at her notes before the speech.

336. grow out of

He grew out of his old clothes quickly.

337. hand back to

The teacher handed back the corrected tests.

338. head for

We headed for the nearest shelter.

339. help out with

Can you help out with the decorations?

340. hold on to

Hold on to your tickets until the end.

341. jump in on

He jumped in on the conversation unexpectedly.

342. keep at

Keep at your goals even when it's hard.

343. kick off with

The meeting kicked off with a welcome speech.

344. laugh off as

He laughed it off as a joke.

345. leave behind in

I left my notebook behind in class.

346. link to

This idea links to our previous discussion.

347. lock out of

I got locked out of my room again.

348. look back on

We often look back on our school memories.

349. make off with

The thief made off with the jewelry.

350. mark down for

She was marked down for spelling errors.

351. meet with

The proposal met with strong opposition.

352. nod at

She nodded at her friend across the room.

353. object over

They objected over the unfair grading policy.

354. pass by

I saw him pass by the school gate.

355. pay off for

All that hard work paid off for her in the end.

356. pick up on

She picked up on the change in his tone.

357. plead with

He pleaded with the officer for more time.

358. point toward

The arrows point toward the exit.

359. pull away from

The car pulled away from the traffic light quickly.

360. push for

The committee pushed for more library funding.

361. put aside for

She put aside some money for emergencies.

362. reach into

He reached into his bag to get the notebook.

363. reason with

It's hard to reason with someone who's angry.

364. reflect on

She reflected on her career choices.

365. result from

The injury resulted from careless handling.

366. roll up to

He rolled up to the event in a fancy car.

367. run across

I ran across an old letter in the drawer.

368. see through

She saw through his lies immediately.

369. settle into

They quickly settled into their new home.

370. shine on

The sun shone on the lake beautifully.

371. shut off from

He shut himself off from everyone after the news.

372. sign off on

The manager signed off on the final budget.

373. sleep through

I slept through the entire movie!

374. speak out against

The student spoke out against bullying.

375. speed up for

The bus sped up for the green signal.

376. split up with

She split up with her partner last year.

377. stare at

Don't stare at people; it's rude.

378. step back from

He stepped back from the deal to reconsider.

379. step in for

She stepped in for her colleague at the last minute.

380. stop by at

I'll stop by at the shop after class.

381. struggle through

They struggled through the difficult task together.

382. subscribe for

We subscribed for a monthly newspaper.

383. swim against

They swam against the current with effort.

384. switch over to

He switched over to a different subject in college.

385. talk over with

You should talk it over with your parents.

386. tear down for

The old building was torn down for renovation.

387. team up with

He teamed up with his friend for the competition.

388. tell on

He told on his classmates for breaking the rules.

389. think ahead to

Start thinking ahead to your final exams.

390. tire of

She never tires of reading detective stories.

391. touch on

The teacher briefly touched on global warming.

392. trade in for

He traded in his old phone for a new one.

393. trip over

I tripped over the carpet.

394. turn off at

Turn off at the next signal.

395. veer off from

The car veered off from the road suddenly.

396. vote out of

The leader was voted out of office.

397. wake up with

She woke up with a sore throat.

398. warm up before

You should warm up before exercising.

399. work through

They worked through the night to finish the project.

400. wrap up with

Let's wrap up with a short quiz.

401. aim at

The lesson aims at improving vocabulary.

402. apply to

She applied to several universities.

403. arrive at

We arrived at the station on time.

404. ask for
He asked for a glass of water.

405. back up from
She backed up from the angry dog.

406. believe about
What do you believe about the afterlife?

407. benefit from
Students benefit from regular practice.

408. bump against
I bumped against the wall in the dark.

409. call for
This calls for celebration!

410. care about
She genuinely cares about her students.

411. cling to
The child clung to her mother.

412. comment about
He commented about the new rule.

413. compliment on
The teacher complimented her on her neat work.

414. confuse with
I always confuse him with his twin.

415. contribute for
We contributed for the school trip.

416. cope with
She's learning to cope with pressure.

417. crash into
The cyclist crashed into a pole.

418. date back to
The temple dates back to the 12th century.

419. deal with
We'll deal with that problem tomorrow.

420. depend upon
We depend upon clean water to survive.

421. differ on
They differ on many political views.

422. disagree on
We disagree on how to solve the issue.

423. draw on

The essay draws on multiple sources.

424. dream of

I dream of becoming a writer.

425. engage in

Students should engage in group discussions.

426. escape through

The thief escaped through the back door.

427. feel for

I really feel for people who are struggling.

428. fit in with

He doesn't fit in with this group.

429. get back from

She just got back from a trip.

430. glance over

I glanced over the newspaper headlines.

431. grumble about

He grumbled about the food in the cafeteria.

432. guard against

We must guard against fraud.

433. hear from

I haven't heard from her in weeks.

434. improve on

You should improve on your spelling.

435. insist upon

They insisted upon a formal apology.

436. interfere with

Loud music interferes with concentration.

437. investigate into

The police will investigate into the matter.

438. laugh with

We laughed with joy when we won.

439. leave for

She left for the airport at dawn.

440. long to

He longed to see his childhood friend.

441. mention to

I mentioned the issue to the teacher.

442. object to
He objected to the proposal.
443. pay attention to
Please pay attention to the instructions.
444. pray to
They prayed to God for rain.
445. provide with
The school provides students with books.
446. react against
The community reacted against the new policy.
447. refer back to
Refer back to your notes before the test.
448. reply to
She replied to the message quickly.
449. reside at
They reside at a new address now.
450. result in
Poor planning often results in failure.
451. run after
The dog ran after the ball.
452. settle for
She settled for a used car instead of a new one.
453. show off to
He showed off his skills to the class.
454. sign in at
Don't forget to sign in at the front desk.
455. sort out with
I need to sort out the problem with him.
456. stand against
They stood against corruption.
457. stay away from
Stay away from junk food.
458. stick around for
We stuck around for the results.
459. stumble upon
I stumbled upon an old diary in the attic.
460. succeed at
She succeeded at her first attempt.

461. switch back to

Let's switch back to the original plan.

462. tap into

We need to tap into our creativity.

463. tear up over

She teared up over the emotional story.

464. tell off for

He was told off for being rude.

465. think ahead about

We should think ahead about the next step.

466. toy with

He toyed with the idea of studying abroad.

467. track down

The detective tracked down the missing person.

468. trip over

I tripped over the rug in the hallway.

469. tune out of

He tuned out of the conversation.

470. turn in to

She turned in to the police station.

471. urge on

The fans urged the team on loudly.

472. vie for

The teams are vying for the championship.

473. volunteer for

He volunteered for the cleanup drive.

474. walk in on

She walked in on her brother dancing.

475. wander around

We wandered around the city center.

476. warn against

Doctors warn against eating too much sugar.

477. wash up after

She washed up after dinner.

478. wish for

I wish for a peaceful world.

479. wonder about

He wondered about the meaning of life.

480. work under

She works under a very strict boss.

481. wrap around

He wrapped a scarf around his neck.

482. write down on

Write your name down on the sheet.

483. yield to

He finally yielded to temptation.

484. zone in on

The speaker zoned in on the main issue.

485. zoom through

We zoomed through the revision quickly.

486. account to

You must account to your manager.

487. adjust to

It took time to adjust to the new place.

488. agree upon

The terms were agreed upon by both sides.

489. argue over

They argued over who was right.

490. attach to

The file is attached to the email.

491. base on

The movie is based on real events.

492. belong with

These shoes belong with your blue dress.

493. bother with

Don't bother with minor details.

494. call upon

The teacher called upon Rahul to answer.

495. cap off with

The evening was capped off with fireworks.

496. check over for

Check over your answers for mistakes.

497. comply with

You must comply with the rules.

498. cut in on

She cut in on our conversation.

499. deal out to
The cards were dealt out to the players.
500. depart for
They departed for London last night.

Adjective + Preposition Collocations

1. afraid of
She is afraid of snakes.
2. angry with
He was angry with his brother for lying.
3. anxious about
They are anxious about the exam results.
4. ashamed of
She felt ashamed of her rude behavior.
5. aware of
Are you aware of the new rules?
6. bad at
I'm bad at remembering names.
7. bored with
He was bored with the lecture.
8. capable of
She is capable of leading the team.
9. careful with
Be careful with that glass — it's fragile.
10. certain about
I'm certain about my answer.
11. clever at
He is clever at solving puzzles.
12. close to
I'm very close to my cousins.
13. concerned about
Parents are concerned about their children's safety.
14. confident of
She is confident of winning the match.
15. connected to
This computer is connected to the printer.

16. content with

He is content with his simple life.

17. crazy about

She's crazy about chocolate.

18. curious about

The child is curious about everything.

19. different from

This book is different from the movie.

20. disappointed in

The teacher was disappointed in the class.

21. disgusted with

I was disgusted with the mess in the kitchen.

22. dissatisfied with

She was dissatisfied with the service.

23. enthusiastic about

He's enthusiastic about the new project.

24. excited about

They are excited about the school trip.

25. familiar with

Are you familiar with this software?

26. famous for

The city is famous for its temples.

27. fond of

He's fond of classical music.

28. friendly to

The new student is friendly to everyone.

29. frightened of

She's frightened of the dark.

30. full of

The box was full of toys.

31. furious about

He was furious about the delay.

32. generous to

She is generous to her friends.

33. good at

He's good at drawing.

34. grateful for

We're grateful for your help.

35. guilty of

The man was found guilty of theft.

36. happy about

I'm happy about your success.

37. honest with

Be honest with your teacher.

38. impressed by

We were impressed by her talent.

39. interested in

I'm interested in learning Spanish.

40. jealous of

She's jealous of her sister's success.

41. keen on

He's keen on sports.

42. kind to

Always be kind to animals.

43. late for

She was late for school.

44. married to

He is married to a doctor.

45. nervous about

I'm nervous about the interview.

46. opposed to

They are opposed to the idea.

47. patient with

Teachers must be patient with students.

48. pleased with

She was pleased with the gift.

49. polite to

He was polite to the guests.

50. proud of

We're proud of our achievements

51. ready for

She is ready for the exam.

52. related to

Is this topic related to the environment?

53. relevant to

Your question is not relevant to the discussion.

54. responsible for

He is responsible for organizing the event.

55. rude to

Don't be rude to your elders.

56. sad about

She felt sad about missing the show.

57. satisfied with

We're satisfied with the results.

58. scared of

The child is scared of loud noises.

59. sensitive to

This skin cream is sensitive to sunlight.

60. serious about

He is serious about his career.

61. shocked at

We were shocked at the news.

62. sick of

I'm sick of eating the same food every day.

63. similar to

This dress is similar to the one I bought last year.

64. sorry for

I'm sorry for being late.

65. sure of

Are you sure of your answer?

66. surprised at

They were surprised at his reaction.

67. suspicious of

The teacher was suspicious of his excuse.

68. terrified of

She is terrified of spiders.

69. thankful for

I'm thankful for your support.

70. tired of

He's tired of doing the same job.

71. typical of

That behavior is typical of teenagers.

72. upset about

She's upset about the argument.

73. useful for

This book is useful for students.

74. weak in

He's weak in math but strong in science.

75. wrong about

You were wrong about the date.

76. accustomed to

He is accustomed to waking up early.

77. amazed at

I was amazed at her performance.

78. annoyed with

She was annoyed with her brother.

79. attached to

The child is attached to his blanket.

80. aware about

She is aware about the latest trends.

81. bitter about

He's still bitter about losing the match.

82. blind to

They were blind to the real issue.

83. careless about

You're too careless about your belongings.

84. concerned with

The article is concerned with climate change.

85. connected with

He's connected with many famous people.

86. crazy for

The kids are crazy for ice cream.

87. depressed about

She's depressed about her job loss.

88. doubtful about

He's doubtful about the results.

89. eager for

The children are eager for summer vacation.

90. eligible for

You are eligible for the scholarship.

91. envious of

She's envious of her sister's success.

92. faithful to

He has always been faithful to his principles.

93. familiar to

Her face looks familiar to me.

94. free from

The document is free from errors.

95. grateful to

I'm grateful to my parents for their support.

96. happy with

He's happy with his new job.

97. honest about

Be honest about your feelings.

98. immune to

Some people are immune to certain viruses.

99. involved in

He's involved in many social activities.

100. kind towards

The teacher is kind towards all students.

101. keen for

She's keen for a chance to study abroad.

102. lucky at

He was lucky at winning the raffle.

103. mean to

That was mean to your younger brother.

104. nervous of

He's nervous of speaking in public.

105. offended by

She felt offended by his remark.

106. open to

The school is open to suggestions.

107. optimistic about

They're optimistic about the outcome.

108. pessimistic about

He's pessimistic about getting the job.

109. polite with

Always be polite with strangers.

110. popular with

She's popular with her classmates.

111. prepared for

Are you prepared for the exam?

112. prone to

He's prone to headaches.

113. qualified for

She's qualified for the scholarship.

114. quiet about

He's quiet about his personal life.

115. reconciled with

She's reconciled with her old friend.

116. related with

Stress is related with poor sleep.

117. reliant on

They're reliant on outside funding.

118. remorseful for

He was remorseful for his behavior.

119. safe from

The documents are safe from damage.

120. scared about

He's scared about the surgery.

121. shy around

She's shy around new people.

122. skilled in

He's skilled in photography.

123. slow at

She's slow at solving math problems.

124. sorry about

I'm sorry about your loss.

125. strict with

The teacher is strict with latecomers.

126. successful in

He's successful in his business.

127. superior to

This model is superior to the older one.

128. supportive of

Her family is very supportive of her dreams.

129. sure about

Are you sure about your answer?

130. sympathetic towards

He's always sympathetic towards the poor.

131. thankful to

I'm thankful to my mentor.

132. tired from

She's tired from working all day.

133. troubled by

He's troubled by the recent events.

134. uncertain about

I'm uncertain about my future plans.

135. unfamiliar with

He's unfamiliar with the new policy.

136. unhappy about

She's unhappy about the changes.

137. unwilling to

He's unwilling to compromise.

138. upset with

I'm upset with how things turned out.

139. used to

She's used to waking up early.

140. worried about

They're worried about their exams.

141. zealous for

He's zealous for justice.

142. vulnerable to

Old people are vulnerable to illness.

143. ready to

I'm ready to help you anytime.

144. ashamed for

He felt ashamed for shouting at her.

145. bad for

Too much sugar is bad for you.

146. close with

I'm very close with my parents.

147. free to

You're free to ask questions.

148. honest to

She's always honest to her friends.

149. mad at

She's mad at him for forgetting her birthday.

150. sensitive about

He's sensitive about his accent.

CHAPTER EIGHTEEN

PREPOSITION USAGE IN ENGLISH

Definition of Preposition:

A **preposition** is a word that shows the **relationship** between a **noun (or pronoun)** and other words in a sentence. It often indicates **direction, location, time,** or introduces an **object.**
Common Uses of Prepositions:

1. **Direction**

   - *He walked **to** the market.*
   - *She ran **into** the room.*

2. **Location / Place**

   - *The book is **on** the table.*
   - *She lives **in** London.*
   - *The keys are **under** the cushion.*

3. **Time**

   - *I was born **in** July.*
   - *He arrived **at** 5 PM.*
   - *We'll meet **on** Monday.*

4. **Cause / Purpose / Reason**

    ○   *He was fined **for** speeding.*
    ○   *She cried **because of** the pain.*

5. **Instrument / Means**

    ○   *He wrote the letter **with** a pen.*
    ○   *She traveled **by** car.*

Prepositions of Place / Position

These tell us where something is.

1. in – inside an enclosed space
The books are in the bag.

2. on – resting on a surface
The phone is on the table.

3. at – a specific point or location
She is at the bus stop.

4. under – beneath something
The shoes are under the bed.

5. over – directly above (not touching)
The painting hangs over the sofa.

6. above – higher than something
The clouds are above the mountains.

7. below – lower than something
The temperature is below zero today.

8. behind – at the back of
The car is behind the building.

9. in front of – directly before something
The students stood in front of the principal.

10. next to – beside something
The school is next to the hospital.

11. beside – at the side of
*He sat **beside** his friend.*

12. between – in the middle of two things
*The ball is **between** the shoes.*

13. near – close to
*There's a bakery **near** my house.*

14. by – next to or close to
*She is standing **by** the window.*

15. inside – within something
*The cookies are **inside** the jar.*

16. outside – not within something
*They are playing **outside** the house.*

17. onto – movement to a surface
*The cat jumped **onto** the bed.*

18. into – movement inside a space
*He walked **into** the room.*

19. out of – movement from the inside
*She ran **out of** the building.*

20. off – away from a surface
*He fell **off** the chair.*

21. across – from one side to another
*They walked **across** the street.*

22. through – from one side to the other, inside something
*The train passed **through** a tunnel.*

23. around – in a circular direction or surrounding
*They walked **around** the park.*

24. along – in a line next to something
*We strolled **along** the river.*

25. past – beyond or after something
*He drove **past** the school.*

26. opposite – facing something
*The bank is **opposite** the post office.*

27. adjacent to – very close, next to
*The conference room is **adjacent to** the lobby.*

28. beneath – directly under, formal
*The letter was hidden **beneath** the pillow.*

29. below – lower than a point
*The valley lies **below** the hills.*

30. beyond – farther than
*The lake is **beyond** the forest.*

31. within – inside a space or boundary
*He is waiting **within** the gate.*

32. without – on the outside, lacking
*They stood **without** shelter in the rain.*

33. among – in the middle of many
*She was sitting **among** her classmates.*

34. upon – formal version of "on"
*The knight stood **upon** the hill.*

35. underneath – directly under
*The keys are **underneath** the cushion.*

36. amid / amidst – surrounded by (formal)
*He stood **amid** the crowd.*

37. aboard – on a ship, plane, or bus
*We got **aboard** the plane at 9 p.m.*

38. ashore – towards land from sea
*The sailors came **ashore** after weeks.*

39. aloft – up in the air
*A kite flew **aloft** on the breeze.*

40. abroad – away from one's home country
*She's currently **abroad** on a study program.*

41. down – towards a lower position
*He rolled **down** the hill.*

42. up – towards a higher point
*They climbed **up** the ladder.*

43. off of – informal version of "off"
*Take your feet **off of** the table.*

44. clear of – not touching or near
*Keep the area **clear of** clutter.*

45. ahead of – in front of
*The car **ahead of** us stopped suddenly.*

46. level with – at the same height as
*The painting is **level with** the window.*

47. to the left of – on the left-hand side of something
*The library is **to the left of** the auditorium.*

48. to the right of – on the right-hand side of something
*The office is **to the right of** the stairs.*

49. within reach of – close enough to touch or access
*The clock is **within reach of** the chair.*

50. out of reach of – too far to touch or access
*The shelf is **out of reach of** children.*

51. far from – at a large distance
The school is far from the city center.

52. close to – near or nearby
He lives close to the station.

53. in the middle of – surrounded on all sides
There's a fountain in the middle of the park.

54. in the corner of – inside, where two edges meet
The chair is in the corner of the room.

55. on the corner of – outside, where two streets meet
The shop is on the corner of Elm Street.

56. on top of – on the highest part of something
The book is on top of the cabinet.

57. in the back of – at the rear
The luggage is in the back of the car.

58. in the front of – at the front part inside
He sat in the front of the class.

59. in front of – before or outside something
The bus stopped in front of the hotel.

60. at the top of – at the highest point
There's a flag at the top of the building.

61. at the bottom of – at the lowest part
You'll find the answers at the bottom of the page.

62. in the background – behind the main focus
A painting hangs in the background of the photo.

63. in the foreground – the area nearest to the viewer
The girl is standing in the foreground.

64. alongside – side by side
The boat sailed alongside the pier.

65. in line with – aligned or matching
The desks are arranged in line with each other.

66. on the edge of – just at the boundary
There's a house on the edge of the cliff.

67. out in – located somewhere outside
They live out in the countryside.

68. in the shadow of – near something large, often figuratively
The village lies in the shadow of the mountain.

69. over the hill – just beyond the top of the hill
The cottage is over the hill.

70. within sight of – able to be seen from
*The lighthouse is **within sight of** the harbor.*

71. within walking distance of – close enough to walk to
*The hotel is **within walking distance of** the beach.*

72. opposite to – directly across from
*The pharmacy is **opposite to** the school.*

73. in back of – behind (American usage)
*The garage is **in back of** the house.*

74. out front of – in front (American usage)
*There's a delivery truck **out front of** the house.*

75. toward the back of – in the direction of the rear
*The bathroom is **toward the back of** the store.*

76. at the rear of – formal for "at the back"
*There's an exit **at the rear of** the building.*

77. parallel to – extending in the same direction
*The road runs **parallel to** the railway track.*

78. in alignment with – directly aligned
*The window is **in alignment with** the door.*

79. under the surface of – below an outer layer
*There's oil **under the surface of** the ground.*

80. in the vicinity of – near or close to (formal)
*There's a gas station **in the vicinity of** the highway.*

81. throughout – in all parts of
*Dust was scattered **throughout** the room.*

82. facing – directly looking toward
*The balcony is **facing** the sea.*

83. centered on – focused in the middle
*The decorations are **centered on** the table.*

84. set against – placed in contrast or background
*The painting is **set against** a dark wall.*

85. running along – stretching beside something
*A trail runs **along** the riverbank.*

86. perched on – sitting lightly on something
*A bird was **perched on** the fence.*

87. embedded in – fixed firmly within
*Jewels were **embedded in** the crown.*

88. hung on – suspended from
*The picture was **hung on** the wall.*

89. leaning against – resting on something for support
*The bike was **leaning against** the wall.*
90. hidden behind – not visible due to position
*The letter was **hidden behind** the curtain.*
91. scattered across – spread over an area
*Books were **scattered across** the floor.*
92. lying beneath – located under
*The money was **lying beneath** the drawer.*
93. tucked into – carefully placed inside
*The blanket was **tucked into** the corners.*
94. resting atop – lying on the surface
*The book was **resting atop** the pillow.*
95. wedged between – tightly stuck between two objects
*The phone was **wedged between** the cushions.*
96. standing over – located above while upright
*She was **standing over** the sink.*
97. hovering above – floating over
*The drone was **hovering above** the house.*
98. spilling out of – flowing from inside
*Water was **spilling out of** the bucket.*
99. lined up along – arranged beside something
*The chairs were **lined up along** the hallway.*
100. jammed into – crammed tightly inside
*Clothes were **jammed into** the suitcase.*

Prepositions of Time

1. at – for specific points in time
Used for: exact times, holidays (without "day"), and certain expressions
Example: *The train leaves **at** 6 p.m.*
Example: *We open gifts **at** Christmas.*
2. on – for specific days and dates
Used for: days of the week, specific dates, or special days
Example: *I have a meeting **on** Monday.*
Example: *She was born **on** July 12th.*
3. in – for longer periods (months, years, centuries, time of day)
Used for: months, years, centuries, seasons, and parts of the day

Example: *He was born in 1995.*

Example: *We go swimming in summer.*

4. by – no later than a specific time

Used to indicate a deadline

Example: *You must finish the assignment by Friday.*

Example: *We'll be home by 8 o'clock.*

5. since – from a point in the past until now

Used with perfect tenses (has/have + past participle)

Example: *She has lived here since 2010.*

Example: *We've been friends since school.*

6. for – a duration of time

Used to show how long something lasts

Example: *He has studied for two hours.*

Example: *We stayed in Delhi for a week.*

7. during – throughout a time period or event

Used for: naming a time or event during which something happened

Example: *He fell asleep during the movie.*

Example: *No phones allowed during the exam.*

8. before – earlier than a point in time

Indicates something happens earlier

Example: *Please arrive before 10 a.m.*

Example: *Wash your hands before dinner.*

9. after – later than a point in time

Indicates something happens later

Example: *We went out after lunch.*

Example: *The results came after the interview.*

10. until / till – up to a certain point in time

Used to show a time limit that continues to that point

Example: *I'll wait here until 5 p.m.*

Example: *She slept till noon.*

11. from...to – beginning and end of a time span

The seminar runs from 10 a.m. to 1 p.m.

12. from...until – similar to "from...to", more formal

He worked here from 2005 until 2015.

13. up to – indicating the maximum time

You can stay up to midnight.

14. throughout – from the beginning to the end of a period

It rained throughout the day.

15. over – during a period of time

*We discussed the issue **over** lunch.*

16. within – before the end of a specific time

*Please submit your form **within** two days.*

17. as of – starting from a specific time

*The rule is effective **as of** January 1ˢᵗ.*

18. ago – a time in the past from now

*She arrived two hours **ago**.*

19. by the time – no later than a particular moment

***By the time** we arrived, the movie had started.*

20. in time – early enough

*He arrived just **in time** for the meeting.*

21. on time – exactly at the planned time

*The train left **on time**.*

22. at the moment – currently

*I'm busy **at the moment**.*

23. at that time – referring to a specific past time

*We didn't know him **at that time**.*

24. at the beginning of – the start of something

*We met **at the beginning of** the course.*

25. at the end of – the conclusion of something

*There will be a quiz **at the end of** the lesson.*

26. until now – up to the present

*We haven't received any complaints **until now**.*

27. till now – same as "until now" (more informal)

*Everything was fine **till now**.*

28. at night – in the nighttime

*I usually read **at night**.*

29. in the morning – specific part of the day

*She jogs **in the morning**.*

30. in the afternoon – middle part of the day

*Let's meet **in the afternoon**.*

31. in the evening – later part of the day

*They go for a walk **in the evening**.*

32. at dawn – early morning when the sun rises

*We left **at dawn** to reach early.*

33. at dusk – the time when the sun sets

*Birds return to their nests **at dusk**.*

34. at noon – 12 p.m. exactly
*Lunch is served **at noon**.*

35. at midnight – 12 a.m. exactly
*The train arrives **at midnight**.*

36. during the night – at some time in the night
*There was a storm **during the night**.*

37. for now – temporarily
*That's enough work **for now**.*

38. in recent years – during the near past
*Technology has improved **in recent years**.*

39. for a while – for a short time
*Let's rest **for a while**.*

40. at the same time – simultaneously
*They spoke **at the same time**.*

41. before now – earlier than the current moment
*I had never seen her **before now**.*

42. since then – from that past moment until now
*He moved abroad in 2010 and has lived there **since then**.*

43. after that – following something
*We had dinner. **After that**, we watched a movie.*

44. until then – up to that future point
*The report is due next week. Relax **until then**.*

45. in advance of – before something (formal)
*The tickets were sold **in advance of** the event.*

46. immediately after – right following something
*The lights went out **immediately after** the speech.*

47. no later than – before a deadline
*Please arrive **no later than** 9 a.m.*

48. shortly after – soon after
*He called me **shortly after** the meeting.*

49. just before – right prior to something
*I received a call **just before** dinner.*

50. long before – a lot earlier
*They left **long before** the storm began.*

51. no earlier than – not before a specific time
*The gate opens **no earlier than** 8 a.m.*

52. no later than – at or before a deadline
*Submit your report **no later than** Friday.*

53. not until – emphasizes something won't happen before a certain time

*He didn't arrive **until** midnight.*

54. ever since – continuously from a point in the past

*She's been working here **ever since** 2010.*

55. right after – immediately following

*Call me **right after** class.*

56. anytime after – at any point beyond a given time

*You can call me **anytime after** 6.*

57. soon after – a little time later

*They got married **soon after** graduation.*

58. a long time ago – far back in the past

*Dinosaurs lived **a long time ago**.*

59. in the meantime – in the time between two actions

*The show starts at 6. **In the meantime**, let's eat.*

60. at present – now, currently (formal)

*She is not available **at present**.*

61. until now – up to this moment

*We had no issues **until now**.*

62. till now – same as "until now", more informal

*Everything was perfect **till now**.*

63. at first – in the beginning

***At first**, I didn't understand the topic.*

64. at last – finally

***At last**, we reached the top of the hill.*

65. just in time – exactly at the right moment

*He arrived **just in time** for the test.*

66. not in time – too late

*She didn't finish **in time** to submit it.*

67. since then – from that past point until now

*He left town in 2005 and hasn't returned **since then**.*

68. up till now – until the current time

*We haven't had a meeting **up till now**.*

69. before that – at a time earlier than a specific moment

*He had never traveled **before that**.*

70. at all times – always

*Visitors must wear ID badges **at all times**.*

71. at every opportunity – whenever possible

*She practices her speech **at every opportunity**.*

72. as soon as – immediately when

*Call me **as soon as** you arrive.*

73. by then – before that future or past time

*I'll be home **by then**.*

74. after that – at a later point

*We went to the mall. **After that**, we had dinner.*

75. just before – right before something

*She left **just before** the bell rang.*

76. immediately before – directly preceding

*We had lunch **immediately before** the meeting.*

77. in due time – at the right or expected time

*Your efforts will be rewarded **in due time**.*

78. from that moment on – starting from a specific time

From that moment on, everything changed.

79. over time – gradually, through the passage of time

*Things improved **over time**.*

80. in the long run – eventually, after a long time

*It will benefit you **in the long run**.*

81. in the short term – for a short period

*This plan works **in the short term**.*

82. up to now – until this point

*We've done well **up to now**.*

83. on the eve of – just before something important

*He spoke **on the eve of** the election.*

84. in recent times – lately

*Crime has decreased **in recent times**.*

85. within days – a few days later

*The parcel arrived **within days**.*

86. within a year – inside a year's time

*They built the house **within a year**.*

87. about to – very close to happening

*The concert is **about to** start.*

88. not long after – soon after

*He moved to Canada **not long after** college.*

89. on the hour – at every exact hour

*The clock chimes **on the hour**.*

90. once in a while – occasionally

*We go hiking **once in a while**.*

91. every now and then – from time to time
*I call my cousins **every now and then**.*

92. quarter past – 15 minutes after the hour
*The meeting started at **quarter past** ten.*

93. half past – 30 minutes after the hour
*Let's meet at **half past** three.*

94. quarter to – 15 minutes before the hour
*She arrived at **quarter to** five.*

95. around – approximately (time)
*We'll leave **around** noon.*

96. by nightfall – before it gets dark
*We reached the village **by nightfall**.*

97. late in the day – near the end of the day
*We finished the work **late in the day**.*

98. early in the morning – soon after waking
*I exercise **early in the morning**.*

99. for hours – a long time
*She waited **for hours**.*

100. before sunrise – early morning
*We left **before sunrise**.*

Prepositions of Direction/Movement

1. to – movement toward a specific destination
*She walked **to** the library.*

2. into – movement from outside to a point inside
*The cat jumped **into** the box.*

3. onto – movement toward a surface
*He climbed **onto** the roof.*

4. out of – movement from inside to outside
*She ran **out of** the room.*

5. off – movement away from a surface
*The book fell **off** the table.*

6. onto – movement to be on top of something
*The bird flew **onto** the branch.*

7. toward – in the direction of something

*He ran **toward** the school gate.*

8. from – indicates the point of origin

*She came **from** the market.*

9. away from – moving farther from something

*The dog ran **away from** the fire.*

10. across – movement from one side to the other

*They walked **across** the bridge.*

11. along – moving in a line beside something

*We walked **along** the beach.*

12. around – moving in a circular path or surrounding something

*He ran **around** the playground.*

13. over – movement above and across something

*The plane flew **over** the mountains.*

14. under – movement beneath something

*The rabbit ran **under** the table.*

15. past – moving beyond or by something

*We drove **past** the hospital.*

16. through – movement from one side to another inside something

*They walked **through** the tunnel.*

17. up – movement to a higher place or position

*He climbed **up** the stairs.*

18. down – movement to a lower place

*She rolled **down** the hill.*

19. onto – movement toward and resting on a surface

*The child jumped **onto** the bed.*

20. off of – informal: movement from a surface

*He fell **off of** his chair.*

21. in – movement inside a space

*She went **in** the classroom.*

22. out – movement outside a space

*He went **out** the door quickly.*

23. back to – returning to a place

*She went **back to** the shop.*

24. forward – movement ahead in direction

*Please move **forward** to the stage.*

25. backward – movement in reverse

*He stepped **backward** when the ball came flying.*

26. down into – descending into a space

*They went **down into** the cave.*

27. up into – ascending into a space

*The balloon floated **up into** the sky.*

28. out onto – moving from inside to on a surface

*She stepped **out onto** the balcony.*

29. over to – across to a location

*He ran **over to** his friend.*

30. around to – moving around to reach a place

*We went **around to** the back entrance.*

31. off from – detaching or removing from

*The lid came **off from** the jar.*

32. away to – going far to a place

*He moved **away to** another city.*

33. on to – transition from one place/activity to another

*Let's move **on to** the next question.*

34. across from – positioned or moving opposite

*The park is **across from** the school.*

35. over into – crossing into a new space

*He leaned **over into** the car.*

36. around behind – circling to the back of something

*Go **around behind** the building to find the entrance.*

37. through to – moving all the way to a final point

*We drove **through to** the last stop.*

38. up to – approach until reaching a point

*He walked **up to** the door and knocked.*

39. alongside – moving next to something

*The cars drove **alongside** the parade.*

40. down to – descending in direction or status

*She walked **down to** the river.*

41. out toward – exiting and going in the direction of

*The cat ran **out toward** the garden.*

42. off toward – departing in the direction of

*They drove **off toward** the coast.*

43. out across – exiting and going across a space

*The deer darted **out across** the field.*

44. right into – directly entering something

*He ran **right into** the fence.*

45. straight to – going directly without delay

*She went **straight to** the principal's office.*

46. down into – moving lower and inside

*They slid **down into** the water.*

47. up onto – moving upward onto a surface

*The girl climbed **up onto** the platform.*

48. out through – exiting by passing through something

*The kids ran **out through** the open gate.*

49. back into – returning inside

*He went **back into** the room to grab his phone.*

50. across to – movement from one place to the other side

*We walked **across to** the other shore.*

Prepositions of Cause, Reason, and Purpose

1. because of – due to; shows the reason

*The game was canceled **because of** the rain.*

2. due to – caused by; formal version of "because of"

*The delay was **due to** heavy traffic.*

3. owing to – as a result of; slightly formal

Owing to illness, she missed the meeting.

4. thanks to – indicates a positive cause

*We succeeded **thanks to** your support.*

5. on account of – for the reason of

*He was absent **on account of** a family emergency.*

6. as a result of – consequence of an action

*The road was blocked **as a result of** the accident.*

7. for – shows purpose or benefit

*This medicine is **for** reducing pain.*

8. with a view to – with the aim or purpose of (formal)

*They started saving money **with a view to** buying a house.*

9. so that – in order to

*She studied hard **so that** she could pass the test.*

10. in order to – to achieve a goal or purpose

*He exercised daily **in order to** stay fit.*

11. as – shows cause or reason

*I left early **as** I wasn't feeling well.*

12. since – because; indicates a reason

Since you're here, let's start the meeting.

13. in view of – considering; because of (formal)

The match was postponed in view of the weather.

14. in response to – reacting to something

The law was changed in response to public protests.

15. through – as a result of

He succeeded through hard work and patience.

16. from – starting point or source of cause

She was tired from working all day.

17. by reason of – because of (formal/legal)

He was excused by reason of mental illness.

18. in the interest of – for the benefit or purpose of

In the interest of safety, the road was closed.

19. for the sake of – for the benefit or purpose of someone/something

She gave up her career for the sake of her family.

20. on behalf of – for the benefit of; representing

I accepted the award on behalf of my team.

21. in consequence of – as a result of (formal)

Flooding occurred in consequence of heavy rainfall.

22. in light of – considering current knowledge or facts

The rules were updated in light of new research.

23. for the purpose of – for a specific reason

The room is reserved for the purpose of interviews.

24. as a consequence of – as a result of

The company suffered losses as a consequence of poor planning.

25. on the grounds of – for the reason of (formal/legal)

He was fired on the grounds of misconduct.

26. by virtue of – because of (formal)

She became a citizen by virtue of birth.

27. for fear of – to avoid something bad

He left early for fear of missing the bus.

28. on grounds that – for the reason that

The protest was canceled on grounds that it lacked permission.

29. in order that – to ensure something

She lowered her voice in order that the baby would sleep.

30. out of – motivated by a feeling or reason

He apologized out of guilt.

31. with the intention of – having the goal of

*They met **with the intention of** starting a project.*

32. by cause of – due to (very formal, rarely used)
*The collapse was **by cause of** faulty design.*

33. in behalf of – for the benefit of (US English)
*He donated money **in behalf of** the children.*

34. by means of – using a method or tool
*He communicated **by means of** email.*

35. by way of – as a route or method
*He entered the room **by way of** the side door.*

36. at the request of – because someone asked
*The session was held **at the request of** the parents.*

37. for want of – because of a lack of
*The project failed **for want of** funding.*

38. at the suggestion of – because someone advised
*He changed his topic **at the suggestion of** his tutor.*

39. as per – according to (used in formal/legal context)
*The policy was revised **as per** the new guidelines.*

40. on account that – for the reason that
*He was absent **on account that** he was ill.*

41. in return for – as a response to something given
*He received praise **in return for** his hard work.*

42. in exchange for – something given for something else
*She offered her help **in exchange for** support.*

43. in favour of – supporting a reason or purpose
*They voted **in favour of** the proposal.*

44. with reference to – referring to a specific matter
***With reference to** your complaint, we're investigating it.*

45. in respect of – relating to or for the sake of
*The clause was removed **in respect of** privacy.*

46. for the benefit of – to help someone
*She explained the topic again **for the benefit of** new students.*

47. because – introduces a reason (often followed by a clause)
*They stayed home **because** it was raining.*

48. seeing that – since or considering the fact
***Seeing that** he was tired, we let him rest.*

49. now that – since something has happened
***Now that** you're here, we can begin.*

50. considering – taking something into account

Considering the weather, we'll postpone the event.

51. in light of the fact that – because of the known situation

The event was postponed in light of the fact that attendance was low.

52. as long as – for the reason that, or provided that

You can go out as long as you finish your homework.

53. so as to – with the intention of

She worked hard so as to get promoted.

54. seeing as – informal version of "since"

Seeing as it's late, we should go.

55. now since – combining time and reason

Now since you've apologized, we can move on.

56. for the reason that – formal way to say "because"

He was excluded for the reason that he broke the rules.

57. inasmuch as – because (formal, legal or academic)

He deserves credit inasmuch as he contributed most of the work.

58. out of respect for – caused by the feeling of respect

They remained silent out of respect for the deceased.

59. in the name of – done for the sake or reason of something

They acted in the name of justice.

60. on the pretext of – with a false or weak reason

*He left on the pretext of feeling unwell.***61. for this reason – as the cause for something**

She refused the offer, and for this reason, we contacted someone else.

62. in retaliation for – in response to something harmful

He attacked in retaliation for their insults.

63. in protest against – done as a form of disagreement

The workers marched in protest against the new policy.

64. as justification for – used as the reason for a decision

There is no evidence as justification for this action.

65. under the excuse of – giving a reason that may not be true

She left under the excuse of a headache.

66. in sacrifice for – given up for a greater cause

He gave up his career in sacrifice for his family.

67. in reaction to – responding because of something

Markets fell in reaction to the news.

68. in defense of – done to protect

He acted in defense of his country.

69. as evidence of – used to prove something

*She presented the letter **as evidence of** the agreement.*

70. as proof of – another way to say "to show cause for"

*He showed his receipt **as proof of** purchase.*

71. in answer to – in response to something

*He wrote a letter **in answer to** her questions.*

72. as a demonstration of – showing something clearly

*She donated the money **as a demonstration of** goodwill.*

73. in the cause of – working for a mission

*They fought **in the cause of** freedom.*

74. on account that – for the reason that (less common)

*He was detained **on account that** he lacked ID.*

75. at the behest of – because someone asked or demanded

*The changes were made **at the behest of** the manager.*

76. with respect to – concerning; often implies purpose

*The decision was made **with respect to** public safety.*

77. with regard to – concerning a reason or factor

*There were no complaints **with regard to** the food.*

78. with the goal of – done to achieve something

*She saved money **with the goal of** starting a business.*

79. in the hope of – hoping to achieve something

*He applied for the job **in the hope of** better pay.*

80. with the aim of – similar to "for the purpose of"

*They organized the meeting **with the aim of** improving communication.*

81. in the pursuit of – trying to reach a goal

*She traveled **in the pursuit of** knowledge.*

82. in appreciation of – to show gratitude

*He received a certificate **in appreciation of** his service.*

83. out of necessity – because it's needed

*He worked two jobs **out of necessity**.*

84. in compliance with – following rules or reasons

*The building was modified **in compliance with** safety regulations.*

85. on suspicion of – because someone is suspected

*He was arrested **on suspicion of** theft.*

86. in tribute to – as a mark of honor

*A concert was held **in tribute to** the late musician.*

87. in recognition of – acknowledging achievement

*She was awarded **in recognition of** her contribution.*

88. in accordance with – for the reason of following rules

*The report was submitted **in accordance with** policy.*

89. on condition that – for the reason that something must happen

*He agreed to testify **on condition that** he'd remain anonymous.*

90. as compensation for – to repay a loss or mistake

*They gave her money **as compensation for** the delay.*

91. for love of – motivated by affection or passion

*He wrote poems **for love of** literature.*

92. for lack of – due to not having something

*The idea was rejected **for lack of** detail.*

93. for the need of – because something is required

*Extra funding was provided **for the need of** better equipment.*

94. by demand of – because someone insisted

*The project resumed **by demand of** the community.*

95. under the assumption that – believing something is true

*He acted **under the assumption that** the deal was final.*

96. in expectation of – because something is likely to happen

*They stocked up **in expectation of** a storm.*

97. for convenience – because it's easier

*She ordered online **for convenience**.*

98. for safety – done to ensure protection

*The door was locked **for safety**.*

99. for clarity – done to make something understandable

*He rephrased the sentence **for clarity**.*

100. with cause – for a legitimate reason

*She was dismissed **with cause** for violating policy.*